BUSINESS PLANNING for ENDURING SOCIAL IMPACT

*A Social-Entrepreneurial Approach
to Solving Social Problems*

Root Cause
Cambridge, MA

Published by
Root Cause
675 Massachusetts Avenue, 9th Floor
Cambridge, MA 02139

Design and Layout
Design Studio at Monitor
Two Canal Park
Cambridge, MA 02141

Library of Congress Catalog Number: 2007943147

International Standard Book Number (ISBN)
paper: 978-0-615-18284-1

Printed in the United States of America

CONTENTS

rootCAUSE ⦿

ACKNOWLEDGMENTS

We are grateful to the many people who contributed to the content and development of this guide. Special thanks to Beth Anderson, Kristin Bierfelt, Colleen Connolly, Anand Dholakia, Elizabeth Hunt, Brook Manville, and Julie Zack for editorial review.

A number of the organizations we have worked with also helped us to draw on their experiences to develop this guide:

Laura Robbins
The Atlantic Philanthropies
www.atlanticphilanthropies.org

Robert Chambers
Bonnie CLAC
www.bonnieclac.org

Jean Horstman
InnerCity Entrepreneurs (ICE)
www.innercityentrepreneurs.org

Katherine Freund
ITN*America*
www.itnamerica.org

Marcia Kerz
OASIS
www.oasisnet.org

Maureen Gallagher
Partners for Youth with Disabilities (PYD)
www.pyd.org

Arlene Williams
Project My Time
www.cyitc.org

Susan Musinsky
Social Innovation Forum
www.socialinnovationforum.org

William Straub
TAP-IN
www.tap-in.org

Nancy Devine
Sheila Murphy
The Wallace Foundation
www.wallacefoundation.org

HOW TO
USE THIS GUIDE

Root Cause's approach to consulting for organizations whose primary mission is social impact combines strategy with organizational and leadership development. We work in direct partnership with our clients, leading them through a process of exploration to realize their aspirations.

Our examples reflect our work with nonprofits that have already been operating for several years, and are looking to bring renewed focus and growth to their organizations and activities. However, we believe that business planning is an essential tool for guiding organizational actions and acquiring resources for all types of organizations whose primary **mission** is social impact—nonprofits, government agencies, and for-profit enterprises alike—at any stage of development. With this in mind, we have prepared this guide for four major uses:

1. **A practical introduction to the business planning process.** This how-to guide introduces business planning to nonprofits, foundations, government agencies, and for-profit enterprises whose primary mission is social impact.

2. **A step-by-step guide for nonprofit organizations, or programs within these organizations, seeking to develop a business plan on their own.** The guide will be particularly useful for existing organizations, and we recommend reading the guide in its entirety before getting started.

3. **A primer on business planning for those seeking external business planning support.** Nonprofits, government agencies, and for-profit enterprises choosing to hire external support may use this guide to get started thinking about the selection process, and to prepare to make the most of the business planning engagement.

4. **A college text for social entrepreneurship courses.** Instructors of social entrepreneurship can use this guide to teach students how to create a practical business plan for enduring social impact.

For a glossary of business planning terms, see Appendix A. For a sample business plan for enduring social impact, see Appendix E.

rootCAUSE ⊚

INTRODUCTION TO
BUSINESS PLANNING FOR ENDURING SOCIAL IMPACT

THE PROMISE OF BUSINESS PLANNING

Imagine a day when organizations whose primary mission is social impact — nonprofits, government agencies, and for-profit enterprises alike — use business plans as their road maps. These business plans define organizational focus and strategy; establish rigorous methods of measuring impact; provide guidelines for making data-driven decisions and improvements; and aid in establishing reliable streams of financial and **in-kind resources**. As a result, they facilitate the rapid generation of successful and lasting solutions to a wide variety of social problems, including poverty, domestic violence, unequal access to health care, and the achievement gap in education.

> Imagine a day when organizations whose primary mission is social impact — nonprofits, government agencies, and for-profit enterprises alike — use business plans as their road maps.

The recent boom in the field of **social entrepreneurship**,[1] supported by the change in strategy of a number of national foundations,[2] has begun to make the above vision a reality. The past decade has seen the emergence of scores of new social-entrepreneurial organizations, the most prominent of which include Teach For America, for which Founder Wendy Kopp was recently profiled as one of *U.S. News and World Report's* Top 25 Leaders; Muhammad Yunus's Grameen Bank, which was awarded the Nobel Peace Prize

---

1 We define social entrepreneurship as the practice of responding to **market failures** with transformative, financially sustainable innovations aimed at solving social problems. Market failure occurs when the cost of a good or service is higher than the price that individuals are able or willing to pay, yet the social benefits from that good or service make availability worthwhile for maintaining a healthy, productive society. For a full discussion of social entrepreneurship and the unique way in which it responds to market failures, see Andrew Wolk, "Social Entrepreneurship and Government," December 2007, in the U.S. Small Business Administration's annual *Report to the President*, available at www.rootcause.org.

2 Sometimes referred to as venture or engaged philanthropy, this new funding strategy combines grant making and management assistance for nonprofit social entrepreneurs. Some of the groups best known for this approach include The Atlantic Philanthropies, Edna McConnell Clark Foundation, New Profit Inc., Robert Wood Johnson Foundation, Roberts Enterprise Development Fund, Robin Hood Foundation, the Skoll Foundation, Venture Philanthropy Partners, and the Wallace Foundation.

for 2006; and Benetech, for which founder Jim Fructerman received a "genius" award from the MacArthur Foundation. These organizations are demonstrating a unique way of responding to social problems that draws on the kind of private-sector strategic thinking that business planning facilitates. What social-entrepreneurial initiatives have in common, and what business planning can help to apply, can be characterized by the following four principles:

- Identifying new *opportunities* within a particular social problem

- Developing *innovations* that lead to promising new approaches

- Demonstrating *accountability* by regularly measuring performance and impact

- Securing predictable revenue sources that achieve **financial sustainability**

Whether you are encountering the term "social entrepreneur" for the first time or you are a veteran in the field, business planning is the essential tool for applying these principles to social problem solving. A good business planning process produces an in-depth understanding of a target social problem that results in identifying *opportunities* that exist to address it. This process also articulates the *innovations* that will help to create promising new approaches. The final product, a complete business plan, demonstrates a commitment to *accountability* by including a rigorous measurement system for assessing and improving performance. It also includes a plan for achieving *financial sustainability*,[3] which ties funding to results and helps to attract funders who seek to invest and re-invest in organizations that demonstrate a clear path to enduring social impact. For this reason, we will use the term **social impact investor** throughout this guide to refer to anyone who provides resources to fund a business plan for enduring social impact.

> Whether you are encountering the term "social entrepreneur" for the first time or you are a veteran in the field, business planning is the essential tool for applying the principles of opportunity, innovation, accountability, and financial sustainability to social problem solving.

---

3 We will discuss the process of achieving financial sustainability in more detail in step three.

To illustrate the promise of business planning, let's consider the experience of ITNAmerica™, a nonprofit organization offering a safe, sustainable, consumer-oriented transportation service for older drivers. In 2005, Executive Director Katherine Freund received funding from The Atlantic Philanthropies, the Great Bay Foundation for Social Entrepreneurs, and the Sam L. Cohen Foundation to develop a business plan that would enable her 10-year-old Portland, Maine–based program to increase its impact in addressing the lack of transportation options for seniors in the United States. Through business planning, the organization explored opportunities to expand its flagship program in Portland to other cities, and it articulated the innovations that helped make the organization's approach unique.

Business planning is an important tool for organizations developing and scaling solutions to social problems and for the organizations that invest in them.

The final business plan included a measurement system to provide the organization with data to demonstrate the current and future impact of the model, while continuing to improve upon it. It also outlined a financial sustainability plan, including steps to raise the $5.4 million cost of the plan over five years. Within just three months of completing its business plan, the organization secured $3.5 million, putting ITNAmerica well on its way to the mix of reliable revenue sources necessary for long-term financial sustainability. As of August 2007, ITNAmerica was operating services in Portland, Maine; Charleston, South Carolina; Santa Monica, California; the Quad Cities of Iowa and Illinois; and Orlando, Florida—with preparations underway to start programs in ten additional cities.

Business planning constitutes an important tool not only for organizations seeking to develop and scale solutions for addressing social problems, but also for the organizations that invest in them. For example, The Wallace Foundation relies on business planning to guide its grant making and ultimately amplify the impact of its current efforts to promote arts learning and out-of-school learning opportunities in Boston, Chicago, Dallas, New York, Providence, and Washington, D.C. The foundation provides support to a range of organizations—including arts and cultural institutions, community-based organizations, and public agencies—generally beginning with funding for a planning process, which includes the development of a business plan. Wallace considers the planning phase of its grants as a means of engaging public and private leadership, gathering necessary facts, and helping the city determine the best way to achieve sustained, citywide impact. Wallace then decides whether to make substantial, multi-year investments—based on the business plan's commitment to innovation and accountability, and on the quality of its financial sustainability plan.

The promise of business planning is quite simple: it ensures that organizations and their social impact investors are working together to address their target social problems with approaches guided by the principles of opportunity, innovation, accountability, and financial sustainability. With a business plan serving as a road map, organizations and their social impact investors can communicate around a common point of reference, while following a clear course of action that will lead to enduring social impact.

Business Plans Serve as Road Maps and as a Means of Communication between Organizations and Their Social Impact Investors

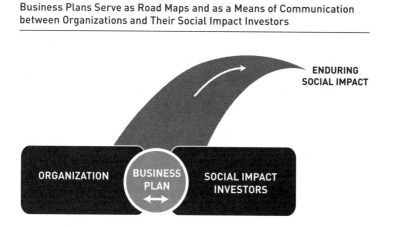

WHAT IS A BUSINESS PLAN FOR ENDURING SOCIAL IMPACT?

In the private sector, a business plan is a document that articulates the steps that a company will take to generate profit, while making a case that will attract traditional investors. It is a road map for carrying out an organizational strategy and a sales pitch in one.

A **business plan for enduring social impact** applies the same strategic rigor and financial savvy to social problem solving. It defines a course of action—generally spanning three to five years—that will guide your organization in generating another kind of profit: lasting social impact. It also shows potential social impact investors how their money will be put to use, including the specific results, or "social returns," that they can expect.

A well-constructed business plan for enduring social impact should tell a clear and compelling story about your organization's target social problem, the unique approach that you will take to address it, and the impact that such an approach will have. Its length will be determined by the amount of space needed to tell that story accurately and convincingly: some plans can be as short as 20 pages while many are about 50 pages. Appendices are about twice the length of the written document; thus a full business plan with appendices is generally 60–150 pages. It should be considered a living document, parts of which you will revisit based on your experience during the implementation process.

A complete business plan will:

1. **Serve as a road map:** The business plan delineates a course of action for your organization's leadership, established governance structure, and social impact investors to follow in carrying out the organization's mission, making day-to-day decisions, and ultimately creating enduring social impact.

2. **Support the acquisition of resources:** The business plan will become your most important fundraising tool as you solicit new and returning investments from corporations, foundations, government, and individuals, and seek sources of **earned income** and in-kind goods and services.

3. **Provide a method of measuring and monitoring performance:** A business plan provides a common point of reference for stakeholders outside of your organization. In particular, it will enable board members to evaluate and understand your performance, and it will allow social impact investors to ensure that their money is being used well.

4. **Help to establish partnerships:** The business plan will also become an essential recruitment tool as you identify partnerships and solicit political support from a variety of stakeholders.

5. **Enrich your field:** Finally, the business plan will contribute to the field surrounding your organization's target social problem,

by articulating your approach to the problem in a form that can be shared with practitioners, social impact investors, researchers, and policy makers.

For an outline of a complete business plan for enduring social impact, see Appendix B.

HOW TO...

Understand Strategic Plans vs. Business Plans

Many organizations in the nonprofit sector are more familiar with strategic plans than with business plans. The biggest difference between the two is their scope:

Strategic Plans generally explore organizational values, goals, and objectives from an internal point of view.

Business Plans serve as road maps to guide organizations in carrying out their missions, as sales documents to aid in acquiring financial and in-kind resources, and as a way for you to communicate your progress to social impact investors. Elements of strategic planning are always part of a complete business planning process. Business plans consider an organization's work in the context of the overall needs and opportunities surrounding the target social problem. They also identify the niche that the organization can fill, list the specific strategies that the organization will take to fill that niche, and provide a plan for acquiring the necessary resources to carry out and sustain its work.

WHAT TO CONSIDER BEFORE YOU START

There are four major questions for any organization to consider before starting a business planning process:

1. **Do you have an idea of where you want to go?** A business planning process provides a rigorous framework for developing the best possible approach for achieving your intended social impact. It works best when you already have a general idea of what you are doing and what you would like to accomplish. When this is the case, the business planning process can help bring your organization's future direction into focus.

2. **Are you ready for the demands of business planning?** Business planning inevitably provokes hard questions and requires tough choices, and it is important to prepare yourself for the demands of the process. Along the way, you may uncover the need to

better allocate resources by cutting one program or expanding another. A business plan can also reshuffle organizational responsibilities and roles, or call for major internal cultural change. To reap the benefits of business planning, your organization — including staff and board members — must be open to making difficult decisions and responding to whatever you discover during the process. Additionally, and perhaps most importantly, your organization must be willing to carry out what will inevitably be an ambitious course of action aimed at growth, and a higher level of accountability than you may be accustomed to, once the plan is complete.

3. **Can key staff members make the time commitment?** Business planning also requires a considerable time commitment from an organization's leadership. You will need to consider who will be involved and whether these potential members of your business planning team can commit sufficient time. As a general rule, conducting a complete business planning process on your own requires the equivalent of one senior-level staff person working full time for about 120 days. Of course, in practice, that work will be divided between the members of your business planning team. This team typically includes your organization's leader, other members of the senior management team, one or more board members, and, in some cases, representatives of stakeholder groups who can provide insights in considering the organization's future.

> For organizations considering hiring external support, there are three basic types: university support, project management, and full consulting engagements.

Developing the plan takes anywhere from four to nine months, depending on how much time you will want to devote to thinking through the options and decisions that come up along the way. During that time, the business planning team will meet about every four to six weeks for anywhere from two to six hours, with additional time required between meetings. Your organization's leader can expect additional work between meetings.

4. **Will you plan on your own or with external support?** Finally, you will need to decide whether to develop your business plan independently or to bring in outside support. If you choose to run

the process on your own, it is important to designate a member of your leadership team to lead the process, along with a lead writer and a facilitator. This option is obviously the least expensive in terms of financial commitment, but also requires the greatest internal staff and board commitment.

For organizations considering hiring external support, there are three basic types available:

- **University Support.** Some organizations choose to engage an M.B.A. student or team for guidance in developing a business plan or portions of it. The advantage of this, of course, is that such engagements are inexpensive or free. Given their tight schedules and limited experience with business planning, M.B.A. students tend to be most helpful when you can give them a well-defined assignment. A portion of the business plan, such as the development of the research-intensive "Need and Opportunity" section,[4] is an ideal project.
  Occasionally, business schools also offer free consulting engagements through alumni consulting teams.

- **Project Management.** It is also possible to hire a facilitator or project manager with business planning experience. The project manager will create a work plan, offer expertise, and help your business planning team stay on track—in addition to facilitating some working sessions. The bulk of the researching, analyzing, and writing will be conducted by your team.

- **Full Consulting Engagement.** In a full consulting engagement, an independent consultant or consulting firm directs the business planning process, carrying out the bulk of the research and writing of the business plan, while leading the organization through the decision making that the business planning process entails. Designated staff members from the organization will work closely with the consultant(s) to collect information on the organization and its field, create and review the necessary documents, and make key strategic decisions about the future of the organization. With such an engagement, you are paying for the time saved by your team, in addition to a consultant's or firm's methodology, knowledge, skills, experience, and impartial external viewpoint—which is

---

4 We will describe the "Need and Opportunity" section in detail in step two on page 17.

often essential to making good choices when tough questions arise. A consultant will also bring experience with facilitation, financial analysis, planning and implementation, and writing and constructing a document for an investor audience. Finally, the consultant may also have relationships with potential social impact investors that could prove useful to your organization.

HOW TO...

Know When to Hire External Support

In recent years, a number of foundations have begun to provide support for hiring consultants to conduct a business planning engagement. Since a primary goal of business planning is to secure the resources necessary to implement the final plan, identifying a social impact investor to help fund the process is an excellent first step. Such investors are often willing to make larger investments when they have seen a completed plan. In addition, it is worth keeping in mind that the planning process will benefit from the external, objective point of view that a consultant can provide. This often also lends greater credibility to the resulting business plan.

We believe that deciding on whether to do internal planning or hire outside support should be based primarily on your organization's access to resources for business planning. Consider who in your network may be interested in supporting some or all of a business planning process. Reach out to other organizations that have gone through the process and learn from them how they were able to acquire support.

If you do not think your organization can find the resources to pay for external support, and you have answered yes to the first three questions on pages 6–7, under "What to Consider Before You Start," we recommend using this guide to plan on your own.

THE BUSINESS PLANNING PROCESS

This introduction has described the promise of business planning for enduring social impact, and provided an overview of the considerations required of any organization before embarking on a business planning process. The rest of this guide will explain the planning process in four steps: 1) Planning to Plan, 2) Articulating a **Social Impact Model**, 3) Developing an Implementation Strategy, and 4) Finalizing Your Business Plan & Putting It into Action.

Overview of the Business Planning Process

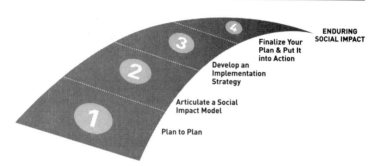

STEP 1
PLANNING TO PLAN

GOAL: Establish your business planning processes, collect existing information, and identify the additional work that you will need to do in
order to complete each section of the business plan.

Step one encompasses the following tasks aimed at getting the business planning process up and running:

1. SELECT YOUR BUSINESS PLAN WORKING GROUP

A business plan working group—the team of people who carry out
the business planning process—has three main purposes: 1) to discuss
and make decisions to support the development of the business plan, 2)
to provide feedback on drafts of the sections of the business plan, and 3)
to decide when sections and the complete plan are ready to be shared
with other stakeholders, in order to aid in winning buy-in of the business
plan each step of the way.

With this in mind, consider who will need to be in the room to ensure
that the plan gets the right mix of perspectives, and the greatest possibility for approval. In most cases, the key players will be easy to identify,
and they typically include your organization's leader, management-team
members, and the board chair if you have one. Ordinarily, five to seven
people is a good target size. With new or very small organizations, however, the working group could consist of as few as one or two people.

No matter how big or small your working group, it is important to define a decision-making process at the outset. The group should commit
to consensus-based decision making, and to keeping decisions final once
they are made.

2. ESTABLISH A STAKEHOLDER UPDATE PROCESS

While the working group will do the hard work of developing the
plan, it is equally important to consider the process through which the
plan will be supported and approved. Start by listing all the stakehold-

ers whose input you value, including your board of directors, whose legal responsibilities to your organization make their approval essential. Also consider anyone outside of your working group who may help to determine your plan's success, such as local politicians, partnering organizations, current and past clients, and members of other leading organizations in your field.

All of your stakeholders should be informed that you have begun a business planning process and of your estimated completion date. You should also keep your stakeholders updated throughout the process. There are many ways to do this. Some organizations choose to send regular e-mail updates, while others stay in touch through one-on-one phone calls, conference calls, or meetings. Many organizations send out drafts of portions of the business plan.

These exchanges with external stakeholders will provide the working group with additional feedback and help to create buy-in—which will be critical when you seek to approve the plan, and when you begin to raise resources and form partnerships with your completed plan. If your business plan is financially supported by a foundation, it is also important to keep the foundation informed of the progress of the plan, whether they need to approve it or not, so that there are no surprises when you submit the final version.

> All of your stakeholders should be informed that you have begun a business planning process and of your estimated completion date.

3. CREATE A WORK PLAN AND APPROVAL DATES

The work plan serves as the working group's to-do list and timeline for the entire process. A good work plan sets meetings as far out as possible, and establishes deadlines for checking in on progress, drafts, feedback, and approval. If you will need board approval, you should also select the board meeting at which you will approve the final business plan. Your work plan will most likely change as you enter further into the business planning process. However, it is important to have it in place—in order to provide focus from the outset, and so that scheduling meetings does not delay progress along the way. For a sample work plan, see Appendix C.

<u>**Don't Skimp on Planning to Plan**</u>

You are guaranteed to run into delays and encounter more difficulties securing investments for your plan if you do not complete each component of step one before engaging in the rest of the planning process.

4. BEGIN PLANNING A ROAD SHOW

Road show is a private-sector term that refers to the practice of securing financing before a company issues a public offering of stock. For our purposes, it is a public announcement of your completed plan that includes meetings with key potential social impact investors aimed at acquiring the investment necessary to implement phase one of the plan. Begin by developing a list of all of your current and potential social impact investors. You should let them all know about your business planning process as soon as you begin. As your planning progresses, send brief updates to everyone on your list. Also make sure that at least one person within the organization — usually the organization's leader — is preparing to pitch the business plan to these current and potential social impact investors at a series of meetings once the plan is complete. We will revisit the road show process in steps three and four, on pages 34 and 54.

5. CONDUCT A GAP ANALYSIS

In order to build on existing information and avoid duplicating work, write up a **gap analysis**. A gap analysis consists of identifying the work that has already been done for each section of the business plan and listing the key areas that require additional work. Begin by gathering all the relevant information for each section of the business plan. This includes your most up-to-date financials, which will allow you to enter the business planning process with a clear sense of your financial situation. Additionally, if your organization has recently completed a strategic plan or possesses an older business plan that needs updating, those documents should inform the new business plan as well. You may also have **organizational and program performance indicators**, background information on your field, or research on the work of your peer organizations. All of this information will help you prepare for the discussions you will hold in future steps of the business planning process, and ensure that all of your organization's planning documents are in sync.

CONCLUDING STEP 1

Before proceeding to step two, make sure that you have established all of the schedules and systems that will facilitate the business planning process. In step two, you will put those systems to use to articulate your Social Impact Model.

STEP 1 CHECKLIST

O Business plan working group

O Stakeholder update process and schedule

O Work plan and approval dates

O Road show list of social impact investors to update and target

O Gap analysis

KEY TO SUCCESS

Work with an Executive Coach

In recent years, some consulting firms have begun including coaching for the leaders of their client organizations, and occasionally other members of the senior management team, as part of their engagements. Such coaching can include training in time management, day-to-day decision making, meeting management, hiring, and how to stay focused on your organization's priorities. Business plans often call for major changes that require the development of new skills. Starting such coaching early in the business planning process, and continuing it during implementation, can help the leadership team to obtain these skills. Whether you are planning on your own or working with a consultant, we recommend seeking out **executive coaching** opportunities as part of the business planning process.

rootCAUSE ®

STEP 2
ARTICULATING A SOCIAL IMPACT MODEL

GOAL: Articulate a model that clearly connects the target social problem with your mission, approach to the problem, **social impact strategies**, intended impact, and vision of what success will look like. This step will ground your approach in the social-entrepreneurial principles of opportunity, innovation, and accountability.

The Social Impact Model articulates your organization's hypothesis about the best way to address your target social problem, as well as the actions that you will take to test and measure that hypothesis, while working toward an enduring solution. As such, it provides the framework that will guide all the work carried out by your organization, at least over the three-to-five-year time frame of the business plan. Other methods for developing a framework for achieving social impact employ a theory of change or a logic model. Root Cause's Social Impact Model blends the big-picture thinking of the theory of change and the step-by-step reasoning of the logic model, and adds a **feedback loop** that enables organizations to continually improve their performance. Once your Social Impact Model is in place, the rest of the business planning process will be aimed at developing a plan for implementing your model and continually testing and improving upon it.

> The Social Impact Model articulates your organization's hypothesis about the best way to address your target social problem as well as your actions to test and measure that hypothesis.

The Social Impact Model is also the key to grounding your approach in three of the core social-entrepreneurial principles: opportunity, innovation, and accountability. Your Social Impact Model will be informed by a need and opportunity analysis, which reviews the context of your target social problem and identifies unique opportunities to address it. As you make decisions about how to further address those opportunities, you will bring into focus the innovations that make your approach unique. Lastly, by clearly stating the logic between your approach and the impact it will have, you will make yourself accountable to the results that your plan predicts.

rootCAUSE ⓡ

The following diagram shows the components of the Social Impact Model at work.

Social Impact Model

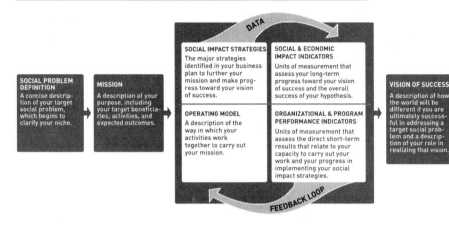

The **social problem definition**, mission, and **vision of success** constitute the foundation of your Social Impact Model; these components will remain the same throughout the time period covered by your business plan. To test your hypothesis about the best way to address your target social problem, your organizational and program performance indicators and social and economic impact indicators will measure your short- and long-term impact. In addition, they will create a feedback loop that will enable you to make course corrections to improve your **operating model** and social impact strategies.

Below, we discuss each of the components of the Social Impact Model in detail, in the order in which we recommend developing them. We'll use as our example an organization for which Root Cause has developed a Social Impact Model that is in its pilot phase.

SOCIAL PROBLEM DEFINITION

The left-hand side of the diagram marks your starting point: articulating the target social problem. To do this, you must conduct a need and opportunity analysis, which will enable you to produce a concise description of your target social problem, and to identify your niche in addressing it.

Conducting a Need and Opportunity Analysis

The need and opportunity analysis is made up of two main components: a study of the trends contributing to the target social problem along with the current work being done to address it, and a description of the opportunity that your organization has identified for putting its unique approach to work. Ultimately these two components constitute the basis of an argument that explains: why now and why your approach?

> Ultimately the need and opportunity analysis constitutes the basis of an argument that explains: why now and why your approach?

A need and opportunity analysis typically covers the following topics:

Market Need: A data-driven description of the social problem in its current context.

Current Trends: An overview of the current social, political, legal, and economic trends affecting your target social problem.

Root Causes: A theory about the root causes of the social problem, based on the research conducted above and a literature review of current debate and thinking by academics, policy experts, and other leaders in your field.

Environmental Landscape: A description of the approaches of other organizations working on the social problem—the competitive landscape—and of the gaps that still remain in addressing the social problem. This analysis of the competitive landscape can begin to illuminate the opportunity on which you are acting and that makes your approach unique.

Barriers: A discussion of the challenges to making progress in addressing your target social problem, in the context of the information described above.

Opportunity: A summary of how the above information frames an opportunity to test a hypothesis about how to accelerate progress in addressing the target social problem, and why your organization is uniquely positioned to do so. This usually includes a brief introduction to your organization's approach as well as information about your organization's progress to date, including recent data about its impact.

In your completed business plan, the results of your need and opportunity analysis will appear as an independent "Need and Opportunity" section. As the first section of the business plan, it should provide a hook that entices your audience to continue reading.

Defining the Social Problem through the Need and Opportunity Analysis

As you conduct the research that will provide you with the information listed above, you will begin to form an in-depth understanding of the aspect of the social problem that your organization is uniquely positioned to target. This will inform the first component of your Social Impact Model: a social problem definition.

Your social problem definition must be based on the research conducted and the data collected in your need and opportunity analysis. It should be specific enough to begin to frame your unique approach to addressing the problem.

Our example organization is an overseas Root Cause consulting client focused on improving the lives of senior citizens. Below are two of the conclusions reached in its need and opportunity analysis.

1. Currently, there is little collaboration and coordination among service providers for the country's senior citizens.

2. Many seniors in the country do not know what services are available to them.

The social problem definition that followed from these and other conclusions is: "the current national infrastructure required to meet present and future needs of people entering their aging years is not adequate and will have a dramatic impact on their lives."

VISION OF SUCCESS

Returning to our Social Impact Model diagram from page 16, the next stop is the vision of success, pictured in the far right-hand side of the diagram. While every organization should also have an idea of the success that it would like to see for itself over the long term, this organizational success should always be envisioned within the context of a broader vision of success: an explanation of what success in addressing your target social problem will look like. As with your social problem definition, the vision of success should come directly from the research conducted in the need and opportunity analysis.

For example, our organization focused on seniors has the following vision of success: "We envision a day when — through collaboration and coordination of government, nonprofits, and the business sector—all seniors, regardless of economic status, will have access to a seamless integration of the high-quality, affordable services they need in order to live healthy and productive lives."

This would be a very different and much less reasonable vision of success if it did not include the phrase "through the collaboration and coordination of government, nonprofits, and the business sector." One organization alone could never hope to meet all the needs of senior citizens, but it could hope to organize a network that makes this possible. This vision of success is clearly based on the social problem definition given above. It also articulates a long-term goal that is ambitious enough to be motivating and inspiring to its stakeholders, yet grounded in the organization's understanding of what's possible.

SOCIAL AND ECONOMIC IMPACT INDICATORS

Next, it is time to begin to develop your **social and economic impact indicators**, which assess your organization's long-term progress toward meeting your vision of success, and ultimately determine whether your hypothesis about your approach to solving your target social problem is working. In some measurement methodologies, the long-term results that social and economic impact indicators measure are known as outcomes. Your social and economic impact indicators will help to ensure that your organization's vision of success is grounded in a set of achievable, yet ambitious, targets—while providing you with the means of generating evidence of your organization's overall impact.

> Social and economic impact indicators will help to ensure that your organization's vision of success is grounded in a set of achievable, yet ambitious, targets.

Here are some social and economic impact indicators chosen by our organization focused on seniors:

- The number of seniors matched to services

- The number of service providers who better meet senior service needs by doing one or more of the following:
  - » adding or making improvements to service
  - » serving a new geographic area or market
  - » improving affordability

Looking at your vision of success, create a list of three to five indicators that will aid you in measuring progress toward your vision of success. In step three, we will describe the process of further developing your list of social and economic impact indicators.

MISSION

The next step is developing your mission statement, which is the second box on the left in our Social Impact Model diagram (see page 16). While many organizations state their missions in very broad terms, we believe that a mission should describe your target beneficiary, the activities conducted by your organization in order to address its target social problem, and the outcomes that you expect to achieve. A mission statement that contains this information will provide an accurate, measurable description of your work, against which you can gauge your organization's progress. It will also help your organization to determine what it will and what it will not do in the future.

A good mission statement will help your organization to determine what it will do and what it will not do.

The mission of our organization focused on seniors, for example, is: "to determine the needs of seniors and link them to necessary resources so that they can lead healthy and productive lives in their aging years." Notice how the target beneficiaries (seniors), the organization's major activity (connecting seniors to services), and the desired result (seniors leading healthy and productive lives) are each included here.

OPERATING MODEL

The next component is an articulation of your operating model—the way in which your organization's activities work together to carry out the mission developed above. To bring your operating model into focus, you will need to conduct an operating model analysis, which will help you to review your activities and begin to uncover opportunities to improve upon current practices.

Much of the information for your operating model analysis will come from the documents that you gathered in your gap analysis, including your organizational budget, descriptions and evaluations of your current programs, and documentation of your current management and staffing structure. You should also plan to conduct interviews with your organization's program directors and management team to gather additional information as you address the following questions.

How would you describe your organization's current mission-based activities? The goal here is to begin to tell a story that explains how the activities that you undertake to carry out your mission work together. Make a list of all of your current activities that address your mission, and think about how you would describe them. For example, do you think in terms of departments? Stages in a process? Or types of programming?

Who makes up your target market? Your target market consists of the primary beneficiaries of your programs and services. Using data generated from your current activities, develop a profile of the characteristics of your target market. These characteristics may include age, geography, and income level.

How are you currently measuring the performance of your programs and your long-term impact? Take stock of the indicators and methods, if any, that you are currently using to evaluate your programs.

What staff positions are needed to carry out your operating model? Develop a list and a short description of the critical roles needed to carry out these activities.

What does your operating model cost? Look at your expense records to determine the cost of your activities, not including your overhead costs. If the activities generate any earned or recurring revenue, gather this information as well.

Your answers to these questions will allow you to create a text document, and possibly a diagram, that explains: how all of your programs and activities work together toward your mission; what groups are brought together by your programs; how evaluation is integrated into your work; how much these activities cost; and how much, if any, earned income you bring in. In your written business plan, this text and diagram will become your "Operating Model" section, which immediately follows the "Need and Opportunity Analysis."

Engage in Action while Planning

The biggest risk in business planning is ending up with a plan that doesn't get put to use. To ensure that your plan won't gather dust once it's complete, we recommend choosing one or two projects that you feel confident you can undertake during the process, without limiting the direction of your business planning. We call this **action while planning**. It can be as simple as testing ways to market to your target beneficiary, designing an application process once it becomes clear that you will be using one, or learning more about how to design a new service for which you have discovered a need. The operating model analysis is one of the first parts of the business planning process that uncovers such opportunities.

To see successful action while planning at work, take the example of Partners for Youth with Disabilities (PYD), which connects youth with disabilities to adult mentors who provide guidance in meeting their personal, educational, and career goals. PYD was interested in developing a business plan to launch a technical-assistance arm of its already well-established direct service program. During the planning process, PYD identified target markets for selling its mentoring approach to other organizations serving youth with disabilities. While it was developing its staffing and financial models, senior staff members began making test sales calls to peer organizations, particularly those that had previously inquired about such a service. These initial calls allowed the organization to practice something new, while testing price points and gauging how much time they would need to allot for such calls. Staff members debriefed members of the working group about the calls, and were able to better set their own sales targets. As a result of the calls, the organization also uncovered several good sales leads to follow up on once the business plan was complete.

Engaging in action while planning will help your organization avoid a major pitfall in business planning — getting caught up in worrying about raising the money before you can implement the plan. Acting on small projects early will help to dispel this fear. It also shows potential social impact investors that your plan is not just an idea, but a course of action that is already underway. Inevitably, organizations that act confidently and build momentum during the planning process have the most success in securing investments.

SOCIAL IMPACT STRATEGIES

We move now to the social impact strategies, which are the major actions that your organization will take to carry out its mission and to strengthen its operating model, while working toward achieving its vision of success.

Basing decisions on the results of the need and opportunity analysis and operating model analysis, many organizations at this stage will determine that they are doing too much. It is not uncommon to end up cutting one program in order to devote more resources to another—or to recalibrate an existing program. The Root Cause consulting client that focuses on seniors had primarily served as an advocacy organization before beginning the business planning process, and had only recently begun helping seniors connect to services. Yet, the organization's need and opportunity analysis uncovered a need for better linking and delivering services to the country's seniors. In addition, the operating model analysis revealed that its existing direct-service programs promised to yield the greatest social impact. As a result, the organization determined to focus on partnering with government to meet seniors' needs, instead of advocating to government. It developed the following social impact strategies:

> It is not uncommon to end up cutting one program in order to devote more resources to another—or to recalibrate an existing program.

- Collecting data on the needs of the nation's seniors through a partnership with the federal government

- Matching seniors with service providers through a membership-driven, technological solution

- Building and strengthening a service provider network through conferences, data reports, and training to help service providers increase the effectiveness, efficiency, and sustainability of their services

- Running a "direct service incubator" to develop new services when a gap is identified

These strategies are all directed toward achieving the vision of success stated earlier: "We envision a day when — through collaboration and coordination of government, nonprofits, and the business sector — all seniors, regardless of economic status, will have access to a seamless integration of the high-quality, affordable services they need in order to live healthy and productive lives."

rootCAUSE ⊚

Look at the Big Picture and Think Creatively

Social impact strategies must be research supported, but don't let this limit you. The key to developing successful social impact strategies is making use of the components of the Social Impact Model developed up to this point to think outside the box. The information provided by the need and opportunity analysis and operating model analysis—along with the organizational focus captured in the vision, mission, and social and economic impact indicators—should empower you to develop innovative strategies that will test your hypothesis and set you on your way to enduring social impact.

ORGANIZATIONAL AND PROGRAM PERFORMANCE INDICATORS

Once you know your social impact strategies, you can begin developing your organizational and program performance indicators. These indicators measure your organization's capacity to implement its business plan, and assess the progress of your activities in carrying out your operating model and social impact strategies; in some measurement methodologies, these types of short-term results are known as outputs. Developing your organizational and program performance indicators will help to ensure that your organization is accomplishing what you intended to in the short term—in order to achieve your vision of success in the long term. When your complete measurement system is in place, these indicators will also serve as a feedback loop that can help the organization make course corrections along the way.

> When your complete measurement system is in place, your indicators will serve as a feedback loop that can help your organization make course corrections along the way.

Looking at your own social impact strategies and the activities they encompass, make a list of three to five indicators that will enable you to measure your organization's overall performance. For example, here are a few of the organizational and program performance indicators chosen by our organization focused on seniors:

- the number of members
- the number of volunteers serving its programs
- the number of seniors assessed

As with the social and economic impact indicators above, you do not need to develop an exhaustive list. In step three, we will describe the process of further developing a list of organizational and program performance indicators.

FEEDBACK LOOP

Keep in mind that two components of your Social Impact Model—the operating model and social impact strategies—are always works in progress, which you will continue to hone based on the results that your indicators reveal. In step three, you will plan for developing a comprehensive self-evaluation system that will include a feedback loop. This feedback loop will establish the systems that will ensure that you regularly return to your operating model and social impact strategies to make improvements based on the data generated by your measurement system. It will also help you evaluate whether your overall hypothesis of how to solve your target social problem is working.

The other components of your Social Impact Model, particularly your mission and your vision of success, should stay the same for the time period covered by your business plan, and should only be revisited when you revise your business plan.

Start Writing Early and Plan for Appendices

It can be quite challenging to capture decisions made by your working group in a written document. Doing so, however, is critical to communicating your business plan to your stakeholders. To give yourself the time to get it right, start writing as soon as you have completed your Social Impact Model. You will be able to complete drafts of three sections of the business plan at this point: "Need and Opportunity," "Operating Model," and "Social Impact Model."

As you draft each section of your business plan, it is also a good idea to highlight the parts of the plan that could be supported by appendices. Generally, a good business plan includes three different types of appendices: 1) data, charts, or additional information supporting various aspects of the plan, 2) documents that show evidence of the organization's past success, and 3) letters of support from stakeholders praising the organization and its plans for the future.

KEY TO SUCCESS

CONCLUDING STEP 2

The work that you have done in step two will turn into drafts of three sections of your business plan: "Need and Opportunity," "Operating Model," and "Social Impact Model." The working group should review and approve the content of all of these sections.

STEP 2 CHECKLIST

○ Draft of "Need and Opportunity" section

○ Draft of "Operating Model" section

○ Draft of "Social Impact Model" section

○ Preliminary approval of all three of the above by the working group

○ Begin stakeholder and road show updates

STEP 3
DEVELOPING AN IMPLEMENTATION STRATEGY

GOAL: *Part One:* Decide on the time period that your business plan will cover, and establish a set of goals for the first phase of that timeline for each of the social impact strategies identified in your Social Impact Model.

Part Two: Determine how you will develop the organizational capacity necessary for implementing your social impact strategies, with specific goals for each of the following sections: Team and Governance, Financial Sustainability, Marketing, Technology, Public Policy, Measurement, and Risk Mitigation.

This step will ground your business plan in the social-entrepreneurial principles of financial sustainability and accountability.

In the previous step, we described the process of creating a Social Impact Model that culminates in a set of social impact strategies that will guide your activities and lead you toward realizing your vision of success. In step three, you will develop your implementation strategy, which outlines the actions needed to put your social impact strategies into action.

PART ONE
Setting a Timeline & Establishing Your Phase One Strategy Goals

BUSINESS PLAN TIMELINE

A business plan timeline identifies the time frame covered by your business plan. The timeline generally has two or three phases spanning three to five years.

Phase one of your timeline constitutes a 12- to 24-month pilot phase for testing the social impact strategies. Your implementation strategy will focus primarily on phase one. Phase two focuses on expanding your organization's reach, and it will have less detail than phase one in your completed plan. Organizations that choose to have a phase three will use this period to provide readers of your business plan with a description of your organization's long-term vision of success.

The chart below provides an example of the phases of a business plan.

PHASE	GOAL
Phase One: **Pilot**	Test each social impact strategy, link the strategies and assess performance of the strategies individually and collectively, and make improvements.
Phase Two: **Roll Out**	Expand the reach of the social impact strategies to provide evidence of a sustainable model and progress toward achieving the vision of success.
Phase Three: **Scale (optional)**	Further scale the social impact strategies, achieve financial sustainability, and test additional innovations.

PHASE ONE STRATEGY GOALS

Once you know your time frame, you can begin to detail how you will put your social impact strategies into action. Setting phase one strategy goals gets this process underway by restating each social impact strategy as a goal, and listing the activities that will lead to accomplishing that goal.

> Once you know your time frame, you can begin to detail how you will put your social impact strategies into action.

OASIS, a national nonprofit providing lifelong learning and service opportunities for older adults, provides an example of how this works. One of the social impact strategies that resulted from the organization's business planning process with Root Cause focused on "increasing the services and tools that the national headquarters, known as the OASIS Institute, provides to local OASIS centers."

In the "Phase One Strategy Goals" section of its business plan, OASIS attaches the following goal to this social impact strategy: "streamline and strengthen the training and other services that the institute provides to the centers."

It then provides a list of the actions that the organization will need to take in phase one in order to meet this goal:

1. Define a menu of all available services, looking at both the cost to the institute and the value to the centers/directors.

2. Develop and implement a training/professional development model with input from the director.

3. Develop and implement services to help the local centers address human resource policies, liability insurance, local contracts, and other legal issues.

4. Develop and implement a standardized annual member survey to be used across all centers.

5. In preparation for phase two, assess performance, determine key success factors, and make improvements based on lessons learned.

As this example shows, your phase one strategy goals should begin to ground your social impact strategies in a set of concrete actions. Returning to your own social impact strategies, rewrite them as goals that you will seek to accomplish in phase one of your business plan. Next, develop a list of the key activities that you will need to undertake in order to meet each of those goals.

PART TWO
Building the Organizational Capacity to Implement Your Social Impact Strategies

The rest of step three is an iterative process dedicated to determining how to build the organizational capacity you will need to implement your social impact strategies. You will hash out the details of putting your Social Impact Model to work throughout this step.

We divide the capacity-building portion of your implementation strategy into seven main sections: Team and Governance, Financial Sustainability, Marketing, Technology, Public Policy, Measurement, and Risk Mitigation. Two of the most critical of those sections, Financial Sustainability and Measurement, will provide you with a financial model and a self-evaluation system in order to ground your business plan in the social-entrepreneurial principles of financial sustainability and accountability.

In the pages that follow, we discuss how to develop each section of the implementation strategy in the order in which it appears in the final business plan, starting with a set of core questions that should guide the development of each. We end our discussion of each section with some suggestions on what to include in the corresponding written section of your business plan. As you did above with each of the social impact strategies, you will want to develop one phase one goal for each section, in addition to a list of actions that will lead to accomplishing that goal during phase one.

TEAM AND GOVERNANCE

? What new roles will you and your staff need to take on?

Are there new staff positions that you will need to fill? If so, what are they and when can you afford to fill them?

If you have a board, how will their roles be affected by the business plan?

Business plans are only as good as the people who can execute them, and this section ensures that you will have the human resources required to implement your social impact strategies successfully. Developing it involves an assessment of your current staff members' skill sets, the new skills that staff may need to acquire, and any new positions that you may need to fill.

First, develop a list of the roles, responsibilities, and skill sets of your current key paid team members, board members, and volunteers. Then compare this with a list of the human resources needed to implement your social impact strategies in phase one. You will likely find that your social impact strategies call for new roles for current staff, in addition to the hiring of more staff members. You should also clearly articulate the board's structure and the roles for each of its members, particularly its officers. In addition, doing the same for any current or future board committees will help facilitate smooth execution of the business plan. Finally, if volunteers are a core component of your operating model, define the role that volunteers will play in implementing your business plan. When you have defined all of the above roles, create a new organizational chart.

Returning to our senior services organization, let's consider the team and governance component of its implementation strategy. As mentioned in our discussion of the Social Impact Model, the organization developed a business plan aimed at building a national network to coordinate the work of organizations that currently provide services to the country's growing population of senior citizens. To this end, the organization called for several changes relating to team and governance. First, the organization rewrote the job descriptions for its three existing senior staff members. In addition, the organization decided to create two new positions, including a director of development, to sustain its new growth plan, which required a significant increase in reliable philanthropic contributions over time. Board members received new, more clearly defined roles under the team and governance plan as well. Finally, the organization developed a plan for incorporating volunteers into the operating model, outlining the specific roles that volunteers would play. As a result, the organization ensured that its team and governance would put the organization in the best possible position to implement its new social impact strategies.

> Business plans are only as good as the people who can execute them.

When you write up your "Team and Governance" section, it should include the roles of current and new staff, as well as your timeline for new hires and a new organizational chart. Also describe your governance structure and the roles volunteers will play. The goal that you list in this section should relate to revised staff and governance structure.

FINANCIAL SUSTAINABILITY

?

How much money will you need over the specified period of time of the business plan?

How will you capitalize — or raise the resources required for — your business plan?

What mix of reliable resources will you seek in order to achieve financial sustainability?

Once you have a sense of your staffing needs, which are typically the most expensive aspect of your business plan, you can begin to determine how much implementation of the plan will cost, and how to acquire the resources. It is important to start early on this section, which grounds your business plan in the social-entrepreneurial principle of financial sustainability. Completing it will be a continuous process throughout step three, as you estimate the costs of all sections of your implementation strategy.

Consider Your Organizational Culture

Every organization has its own unique culture. As you prepare to carry out social impact strategies that will likely involve new hires, you should understand the nature of the culture you've created, particularly the parts of it you want to maintain. One way to do this is to hold a discussion at your next team meeting and identify three to four characteristics that you think make your organizational culture unique. Be sure to discuss your organizational culture with candidates for new positions to get a sense of their ability to adapt to and participate in this culture. This should be a major part of your consideration as you select new hires.

You will work toward two goals within this section:

- **Capitalization:** identifying the total amount of philanthropic investment needed—not including earned income and future funds that have already been committed—in order to execute the business plan and developing a plan for acquiring the necessary resources for phase one.

- **Financial sustainability:** developing a financial sustainability plan, which identifies a reliable and at times diversified revenue mix that will ultimately allow you to predict your annual revenue and its sources with reasonable certainty.

Generally, organizations will require significant initial philanthropic investments, which serve as seed money, before achieving the ideal revenue mix that will bring about financial sustainability. The "Financial Sustainability" section, then, should lay out a **capitalization plan** aimed at getting your organization to the necessary mix of reliable funding streams. (The capitalization plan is what you will begin carrying out with the road show that you began preparing in step one.) In some cases, organizations will achieve financial sustainability by the time they reach the end of the business plan timeline. In other cases, they will still be making progress toward financial sustainability when the time period covered by the business plan ends.

To get started, return to the financials that you gathered in step one, including up-to-date revenue and cost statements. You will also need to know your cash balance as of the last day of the most recent month so that you can begin to develop projections. Then follow the three steps described below:

1. Estimate Costs

Begin by reviewing and making any necessary changes to the types of expenses incurred by your organization. Then estimate the costs for all aspects of implementing your business plan. Phase one will be the primary focus of these projections, since much can change by the time you get to phases two and three. You should estimate phase one costs on a monthly or quarterly basis so that you can pay close attention to cash flow, and phases two and three on a yearly basis. Look closely at the aspects of your business plan that require a significant capital investment, such as technology or hiring additional staff or consultants. It is important to get estimates from trustworthy sources for these types of expenses, in order to make your calculations as accurate as possible.

2. Estimate Capitalization Required

Once you have a sense of the cost of implementing your business plan, review your current and projected revenue to determine your funding needs for each phase of implementation. Begin with your earned revenues, if any, and subtract the estimated expenses for implementation. This is illustrated in the diagram on the next page as Profit/(Loss). You may already have committed philanthropic revenue to list, to which you will add figures for any likely philanthropic revenue. After you've subtracted committed and likely philanthropic revenue, you'll arrive at the capitalization amount necessary to implement each phase of your business plan.

> Generally, organizations require significant philanthropic investments, which serve as seed investments, before achieving the ideal revenue mix for financial sustainability.

The figure on the next page shows an example of this type of calculation. In this scenario, the organization would need to raise $1.3 million in phase one and $6.9 million in phase two, for a total capitalization of $8.2 million.

Sample Calculation of Capitalization Required

TIME PERIOD	PHASE ONE	PHASE TWO	TOTAL
Earned Revenues	$173,000	$662,000	$835,000
Expenses	$3.5 million	$8.1 million	$11.6 million
Profit/(Loss)	($3.3 million)	($7.4 million)	($10.7 million)
Committed Philanthropy	$500,000	$375,000	$875,000
Likely Philanthropy	$1.5 million	$202,000	$1.7 million
Total Philanthropy	$2.0 million	$577,000	$2.6 million
Capitalization Amount	($1.3 million)	($6.9 million)	($8.2 million)

KEY TO SUCCESS

Don't Forget Your Road Show

Once you have a draft of your "Financial Sustainability" section in hand, you will have an idea of how much money you will need to raise. At that point, it is time to return to the list of potential social impact investors that you developed for your road show in step one. Provide these investors with an update, and, if possible, arrange to set up a meeting or invite them to a gathering within a few weeks of the plan's expected approval date.

3. Develop a Plan for Capitalizing Phase One and Achieving Financial Sustainability

Models for operating in a state of financial sustainability differ greatly depending on the type of social problem you are addressing. Yet, all tend to include two fundamental components:

- **Predictable revenue sources:** These are long-term, repeat, and performance-based funding sources—foundation, individual, government, corporate, and fee-based—that your organization believes it can rely on with reasonable certainty.

- **Non-financial resources:** These are skilled or unskilled volunteers, and one-time or recurring in-kind donations that enable organizations to increase the sustainability of their initiatives.

In general, before reaching financial sustainability, nonprofits generate the vast majority of their revenue from unpredictable philanthropic sources—mostly foundation grants that tend not to support the same organizations over long periods of time. Capitalizing your business plan, then, often requires seeking philanthropic and other revenue sources that will move you toward financial sustainability. If your business plan was sponsored by a foundation, this is a good place to start. This is also the primary purpose of your list of social impact investors for your road show—to help you capitalize phase one.

> Your written "Financial Sustainability" section should include the total capitalization required to implement your business plan, and a full set of financial statements.

To work toward financial sustainability, it is important to find ways to develop earned income streams, when possible, and to increase predictable philanthropic revenue. Earned income streams from government fee-for-service and membership fees, in addition to individual donors and corporate partners, are often core elements of an organization's financial sustainability model.

The pie charts below show a sample strategy for shifting an organization's revenue toward more predictable funding sources—such as earned income and individual donors—over the course of four years. Notice the shift away from unpredictable revenue toward earned income, individual donations, and corporate sponsorships; all of these represent funding sources that tend to be more reliable.

FY 2007   FY 2011

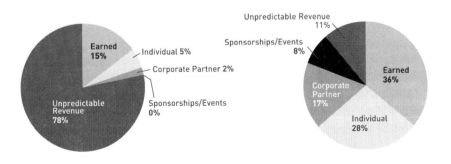

The financial sustainability plan is one of the most important components of the business plan, as it is a powerful fundraising tool. For instance, a nonprofit equipped with a plan for achieving financial sustainability in its third year of operation, through a combination of individual giving, membership fees, and government fee-for-service, has a great pitch for seeking foundation funding. Foundations will see that an investment in the first three years will not only achieve social impact, but also support the organization in reaching a stage in which little or no foundation funding is needed.

HOW TO...

Capitalize a For-Profit Business Plan for Enduring Social Impact

For-profit organizations whose primary mission is social impact tend to be operating in **low-profit markets**, which are not yet developed enough to provide the return on investment generally expected by traditional investors. There are two major financial sustainability models for these types of for-profit enterprises:

1. The organization can achieve financial sustainability by developing a low-profit market into one that will eventually allow the organization to exist as a traditional for-profit company. In some cases, the organization will rely on **patient capital** from social impact investors who are willing to accept below-market returns for an extended period of time as the organization works toward developing a market that will eventually lead to more traditional returns on investment.

2. If it is not possible to advance beyond low-profit-market conditions, the financial sustainability model will continue to rely on this patient capital, which will come from social impact investors who are willing to accept below-market returns for social impact.

The first challenge in capitalizing a for-profit business plan for enduring social impact is that you may have no track record. To win investor confidence, it is important to determine the minimum investment necessary to meet a major milestone that will prove your concept and attract future investments. By investing the least possible amount of money in the first stage of testing your idea, you and your social impact investors will keep your financial losses to a minimum if the venture fails. Many for-profits rely on their founders' own resources at the beginning. As you test the ideas and generate proof of potential profitability, you can seek outside social impact investors more easily.

For-profits face an additional challenge at the outset: many investors believe that organizations whose primary mission is social impact cannot make money. For this reason, it is important to develop financials that show a decent rate of return in comparison to other similar investment opportunities. If your financials cannot show how you intend to make a profit and offer a return to investors, raising money will be a challenge—unless your investors consider the money as philanthropy.

Your written "Financial Sustainability" section should include the total capitalization required to implement your business plan, a full set of financial statements based on the timeline of the business plan, and a description of your plan for achieving financial sustainability. This section's goal should focus on capitalizing the business plan and achieving financial sustainability.

MARKETING

? What standards and systems do you need to put in place in order to communicate your work in consistent and compelling ways?

What types of communications or marketing would best reach your target market(s)?

What are the critical partnerships that your organization should make to ensure success?

Increasing the impact of your organization requires ensuring that the standards and systems are in place to communicate what you do in a compelling way, in order to reach the groups that will help you to increase your impact. These groups include the beneficiaries of your programs, or your target market, and potential partners—including social impact investors, local decision makers, and leaders of peer organizations. To this end, the Marketing section is made up of three main parts: brand and communications, target marketing, and partnerships.

Brand and Communications

In order to develop a clear brand and communications strategy, it is best to start with an audit. This audit is aimed at determining the systems and standards necessary to communicate your approach to creating social impact to others: social impact investors, clients, partners, employees, board members, and other stakeholders. Many organizations choose to bring in a communications consultant at this stage, as the better you are able to communicate with your stakeholders, the greater success you will have in getting them excited about your work. Furthermore, strong communications are essential to attracting new social impact investors, partners, and participants for your programs.

The following list describes what your audit should consider:

1. **Messaging and Brand Standards:** The foundation of a solid brand and communications strategy is consistent messaging and branding. Start by reviewing the documents that your organization uses to describe its work to any of the above groups. Does the way that you currently describe your organization provide people who may not be familiar with your organization with a clear sense of what you do? Does this messaging convey the promise of your work—the vision of success that you are working toward? Does it have the potential to capture the attention of your stakeholders?

   Also, look at the way in which you represent your brand. Do you have guidelines for using logos and colors associated with your brand that can serve as sources to draw on for future documents? If so, do you have templates for memos, slide presentations, job descriptions, and other materials that will ensure consistent branding and messaging—in addition to helping to make the process of creating new materials more efficient?

   Make a preliminary list of your organizational needs based on your answers to these questions.

2. **Communications Materials:** Whether or not you have the above standards in place, your audit should also look at the types of communications materials that you are already using. These may include:

   » A Web site

   » An editorial calendar of newsletters and other publications for communicating to targeted groups

   » An online forum for national communication with the public on the target social issue

   » A conference or event dedicated to raising awareness of the target social issue and positioning the organization as a leader in its field

   » Brochures and other public documents that showcase your organization's perspective on your target social problem and how your solution can make a lasting impact

> » Core media messages, based on analyses of past earned media coverage whenever possible

> » News articles and press releases targeted to appropriate media markets in order to deliver specific media messages

Strive for Sustainability in All Aspects of Your Plan

Organizations tend to think about sustainability primarily from a financial point of view. Yet, a strong business plan for enduring social impact will consider sustainability more broadly. For example, your business plan should enable you to stay on course in the event of leadership change—which may require establishing a succession plan. Another example may be ensuring that the new systems that your business plan establishes become a lasting part of your organization's approach to its work. An organization should also consider sustainability in terms of the political landscape in which you operate. This could mean keeping a close watch on policies affecting your target social problem and staying in contact with politicians. As you develop each section of your business plan, consider how you can ensure that your individual actions will result in a sustained social impact—even beyond the period covered by your business plan.

Which of these items will generate the most benefit for your organization depends on the audiences you want to reach and the resources available to you. An organization setting out to influence its field with a new approach to preventing domestic violence, for example, might prioritize conferences or other meetings aimed at influencing other organizations working on the same issue. An environmental organization working to pass a new pollution-prevention bill might choose to run a media campaign aimed at raising public awareness of the issue and support for the campaign. Organizations focused on building a member base or reaching a community around a particular interest area might center their efforts on sending out an e-newsletter and creating an online forum.

Target Marketing

This part of your Marketing section will identify how you will reach out to your target markets. Depending on your Social Impact Model, you may have numerous target markets. In addition to direct beneficiaries, they may also include volunteers and new cities into which your organization hopes to expand.

It is important to develop a clear profile of each of the groups included in your target markets. Then you can begin developing the strategies that will allow you to reach out to those groups, and to improve upon them as you continuously strengthen the profile of your target markets and utilize your marketing dollars more wisely.

Bonnie CLAC, a New Hampshire–based nonprofit that helps individuals build credit and obtain low-interest car loans, provides an example of a target marketing plan. First, based on its operating model analysis, the organization determined that the clients best positioned to benefit from its programs generally have the following characteristics: they do not have accounts in collection and they have an average annual salary of $20,000 or higher, with at least $300 of disposable income after monthly expenses are paid. With this profile in hand, Bonnie CLAC developed a series of marketing strategies, including increasing client referrals, direct marketing through newspaper advertisements, and direct mail. The organization also began offering its services through partnerships with local corporations whose employees fit this profile, and with organizations that help low-income people with financial planning or job training.

Partnerships

Partnerships are essential to strengthening your operating model and scaling your social impact. Partnerships can also provide access to new markets and ultimately help to better serve the communities that your programs and services are designed to benefit.

Partnerships are essential to strengthening your operating model and scaling your social impact.

With this in mind, determine which areas of the operating model provide the best opportunities for building upon existing partnerships or forging new ones. Then develop criteria for identifying partners in each of these areas. For example, if your operating model requires access to volunteers with legal skills, you may want to seek a partnership with a law firm, and you will want to determine what kind of law firm would make the best partner for your organization. To do this, list criteria that will allow you to compare law firms. At the same time, consider what you have to offer in the partnership—as all successful partnerships provide value for both parties, and you will need to communicate this.

When you draft your "Marketing" section, it should include a list of what you need to get your brand and communications systems ready to carry out your social impact strategies; a description of your target market(s) and how you will reach them; and a description of the areas in which you hope to seek partnerships, the ideal characteristics of your partners, and a short list of current or possible future partners you will reach out to. Your goal in this section should center on meeting the needs identified for brand and communications target marketing and partnerships.

TECHNOLOGY

> **?**
>
> How is your organization currently using technology both for internal operations and for your external work?
>
> Does your business plan's potential to succeed depend on technology improvements?
>
> Where can you find resources to get this done?

A robust technological infrastructure—including measurement systems, contact databases, and proprietary technology that aids in carrying out your operating model—is the single most important factor in expanding the reach of an organization. Making changes to existing technology or implementing new technology solutions often requires hiring an outside technology consultant (unless you have this expertise in-house), in addition to making a significant initial investment. Avoiding these hurdles by passing over the "Technology" section may be tempting, but the rewards of a solid technology plan make it well worthwhile.

> Organizations that devote resources to technology can gain a significant increase in their efficiency, effectiveness, and sustainability, as well as a competitive advantage.

The right technology can greatly increase your organizational capacity, while enhancing your ability to serve your target population, to connect with other stakeholders, and to demonstrate your organization's impact with the data you collect over time. Organizations that focus on devoting resources to technology can gain a significant increase in their efficiency, effectiveness, and sustainability, as well as a competitive advantage.

For example, in developing a transportation service for seniors that operates nationwide, ITN*America*'s leadership realized that the organization required a robust technology infrastructure to manage the service logistics and the community outreach necessary for financial sustainability. The organization built ITN*Rides*™, a customized technology system that uses a Geographic Information System (GIS) and a database to manage all aspects of the ITN operating model. ITN*Rides* became the cornerstone of the organization's social impact strategies for nationwide expansion.

> In many cases, developing a solid technology plan constitutes the only way for an organization to scale.

ITN*America* illustrates an important lesson for organizations engaging in business planning. In many cases, developing a solid technology plan constitutes the only way for an organization to succeed at achieving greater efficiency or to scale a program that is working well. It is simply too expensive to rely on human capital for work that technology could better accomplish. At the same time, it can be challenging to raise money for new technology. Including a technology plan as part of an overall business plan, which clearly demonstrates the link between technological infrastructure and the mission of the overall organization, is often the best way to attract social impact investors willing to support technology improvements.

As you transcribe the decisions made here into your "Technology" section, make sure to include a thorough description of the technology that will aid you in carrying out your Social Impact Model. The goal for this section should state the specific changes you will make to existing technology.

PUBLIC POLICY

? What are the current local or national public policies that relate to your target social problem?

Are there challenges your business plan might face that legislation at the state or federal level might help alleviate?

Is there an opportunity for your model to spread nationally through state or federal legislation?

If an organization or initiative can devote the necessary resources, the "Public Policy" section of an implementation strategy can be critical to achieving large-scale social impact. Even if you decide not to prioritize public policy initiatives, understanding the public policies surrounding your target social problem will provide you with a much greater chance of successfully implementing your business plan. In any work aimed at solving a social problem, there will always be local, state, or national public policies affecting your approach to your target social problem. A good business plan includes a section that identifies key players and policies (current or potential) that would aid your organization in scaling its approach. Ultimately, the public policy portion of the business plan provides a chance to plan for larger systemic change—beyond your organization's ability to have social impact on its own. It pinpoints opportunities for altering the very policies that may help to scale your organization's approach or that may be contributing to the social problems that your organization's work addresses.

As an example, let's consider a policy action taken by ITNAmerica. A core part of ITNAmerica's operating model in Maine was the ability to accept donated or traded cars to use as part of its service, and to sell them to raise money. In the first years after the CarTrade™ program was developed, however, the organization faced a challenge in its home state of Maine: a state law required ITN-Portland™ to accept only a limited number of donated or traded cars unless they met the requirements of a car dealership—a two-bay garage and a mechanic on duty.

> Ultimately, the public policy portion of the business plan provides a chance to plan for larger systemic change.

After researching the issue, ITNAmerica discovered that the state of Maine had made an exception to this law in recent years for nonprofit organizations that accepted used cars as donations and repaired them for low-income people to help them get to work. Appealing to the legislature's transportation committee, ITNAmerica made the case that if helping low-income people was a worthy exception in the interest of society, so was helping older people who wanted to trade their own cars to pay for their own rides. As a result of ITNAmerica's efforts, Maine's *Act to Promote Access to Transportation for Seniors*, sponsored by State Senator Michael Brennan, passed in 2005. It provides an exemption from automobile dealership laws for any public or nonprofit organization that uses automobile donations to provide transportation for older persons, or that takes personal automobiles in trade from older persons in exchange for transportation services.

ITNAmerica's experience demonstrates how to get started on a public policy section. First, conduct research to identify politically feasible public policy initiatives that could help strengthen your operating model, while benefiting other groups as well. Then begin looking into your network to determine how you can build the relationships that you need to start working on the change that you would like to bring about.

Your written "Public Policy" section should describe the public policies affecting your work and how you might expect to contribute to influencing them. The goal for this section should focus on what needs to happen to get this work done.

PERFORMANCE AND SOCIAL IMPACT MEASUREMENT

> **?** What indicators will you need to evaluate and hone your operating model and social impact strategies?
>
> What systems do you need to create in order to ensure that you are measuring your performance regularly and using those results to make improvements to your operating model and social impact strategies?
>
> How will you report your results both internally and externally?

Measuring your performance and social impact is the best way to commit to the social-entrepreneurial principle of accountability, while maintaining a high level of quality and developing a track record that will help you secure new and returning investments. In this section, you will further develop the indicators that you started on as part of your Social Impact Model as part of a comprehensive self-evaluation system that is focused on enabling your organization to assess its own capacity and performance, and to use the results to make improvements to its operating model and social impact strategies.[5] Your self-evaluation system will also test your hypothesis of the best approach to generating enduring social impact. To accomplish this, complete the following actions.

---

5 For more detail on how to create a self-evaluation system, see our forthcoming how-to guide "Performance Measurement for Enduring Social Impact: Five Steps to Putting Measurement to Work for Your Organization" at www.rootcause.org/knowledge_sharing.

1. Develop Your Indicators

Return to the organizational and program performance indicators and the social and economic impact indicators that you began developing in the Social Impact Model.

Organizational and program performance indicators

Remember, some of these indicators will help you to assess your organization's capacity and may include your organizational budget, months of cash reserve on hand, staff size, and turnover. As you begin measuring these indicators regularly, they will provide you with a sense of how efficient, stable, and sustainable your organizational capacity is.

> A self-evaluation system enables your organization to assess its own capacity and performance and use the results to improve its operating model and social impact strategies.

Now think about what you will need to know in order to evaluate your operating model and social impact strategies, to reach your phase one strategy goals. Returning to your Social Impact Model, review these two components and continue to work from the list you already developed. For example, your list may include the number of people served or number of members. Make sure your list also includes indicators that will allow you to assess progress in phase one for each of your social impact strategies.

HOW TO...

Performance Measurement for Enduring Social Impact: Five Steps to Putting Measurement to Work for Your Organization

By developing your own self-evaluation system, you are taking a major step toward ongoing improvement and communication of your impact. Some organizations will choose to take measurement a step further, by hiring a third-party evaluator, such as a market research firm or an academic research team. If your organization receives, or plans to solicit, a significant amount of government funding, we highly recommend third-party evaluation — as it is often critical to securing stable federal or state funding. Third-party evaluation, however, is not for everyone, as it is time-consuming and costly. For most organizations primarily funded by foundations and individuals, a self-evaluation system is the most time- and cost-effective option. If you are unsure about the measurement requirements of your social impact investors, we recommend consulting with a few of them at this stage in the business planning process.

Social and economic impact indicators

These are the most challenging indicators to develop and measure, as you will be looking to test your hypothesis of the long-term social impact you expect your operating model and your social impact strategies to have on your target social problem. Even organizations that are preparing a business plan internally may find it worthwhile to engage an external firm for this section of planning. To build on the list of social and economic impact indicators that you created in step two, try to look at recent research on your target social problem, and select the indicators that are most widely agreed upon. For example, an organization aimed at getting high school students into college would want to know what percentage of graduates of the program go on to enroll in a college or university. Of those, the organization may also want to calculate how many complete a degree and, possibly, the types of careers they choose and the average salaries they earn afterward.

2. Set Targets to Measure with Your Indicators

Whether you are developing indicators on your own or with external help, you will need to set some targets, when possible, against which you will measure your progress. For each indicator, determine your baseline from existing data. Then identify the target that you will be aiming for in the first phase of your business plan or some shorter period of time. If you are developing an indicator with no existing data, you may not know your baseline, so it will be more difficult to set a target; in that case you should make sure you are gathering enough information to establish a baseline and set a target in the near future.

There are two types of reports that will enable you to analyze your data regularly, communicate your progress, and use the data to improve your operating model and social impact strategies: dashboards and report cards.

For example, consider a membership organization that has chosen the total number of members as one of its indicators. Its current, or baseline, membership is 20,000, and it has set a target of 50,000 members by the end of phase one of its business plan. Keep in mind that your baselines and targets will change as you gain more experience during the implementation of your business plan and gain a better sense of baselines in your field and realistic targets for your organization. What is most important is to set them if you haven't already.

HOW TO...

Lead Your Field with a Research Agenda

If your organization is interested in leading your field, developing a research agenda, based on data generated by your self-evaluation system or a third-party evaluator, is an excellent way to do so. You can start by seeking out academic departments or individuals specializing in your field. Most researchers are more than happy to find a new, reliable data set that is relevant to their work. Partnering with researchers often results in published papers, which can provide excellent visibility and credibility for your organization.

3. Establish a Feedback Loop

Once you know what you will be measuring, you can plan for establishing a feedback loop that will help you to make course corrections based on your data. First, your organization will need to decide which methods it will use to gather information—such as surveys, focus groups, or direct observation. Then, you can plan for two types of progress reports—**dashboards** and **report cards**—that will enable you to analyze your data, identify opportunities to make improvements to your operating model and social impact strategies, and communicate your progress and social impact. A dashboard is distributed internally to staff and sometimes to board members and includes measurements to help an organization ensure that it is operating in an efficient, effective, and sustainable manner. Dashboards include all of the indicators selected above. A report card is an annual, public presentation of a subset of your dashboard measures, which allows funders and other key stakeholders outside of an organization to monitor the organization's progress and social impact. Plan to assign a staff member the task of analyzing data and incorporating the data into both types of reports.

To illustrate the importance of demonstrating accountability through regularly published report cards, let's consider the experience of Inner-City Entrepreneurs (ICE), a Root Cause social enterprise that promotes job creation, wealth generation, and community development by helping a diverse group of urban entrepreneurs strengthen and grow their existing businesses. In 2005, ICE released its first annual report card, which assessed its performance in its first two years of operation. The report card's results showed, among other things, that by 2005 ICE graduates had created 77 new part- and full-time jobs in Boston, 59 percent of which were from the businesses' local neighborhoods. ICE entrepreneurs had also increased their sales by more than 13 percent.

By measuring and publishing these results, ICE was able to secure several new funding sources, including a new six-figure multi-year funder who helped to cover the salary of a CEO, a new position aimed at enabling the organization to scale nationally. By the time ICE released its second report card, it was on its way to national expansion, starting with the opening of a second site to serve urban entrepreneurs in Worcester, Massachusetts.[6]

Your written "Performance and Social Impact Measurement" section should provide a complete list of your organizational and program performance indicators and your social and economic impact indicators, along with a chart setting baselines and targets when possible. For all organizations, this section will also include a schedule for measuring and reporting indicators, and a description of how you will establish the systems that will allow you to use the information you collect to make improvements to your operating model and social impact strategies, while communicating your progress and social impact. Your measurement goal for phase one should relate to putting these systems in place, and getting your self-evaluation system underway.

HOW TO...

Address Your Organization's Legal Needs

While not necessarily a section of a completed business plan, legal issues often come up during business planning. To determine what degree of legal advice you may need, consider the following questions:

- Have you explored obtaining copyrights or trademarks for any of your work?
- If your organization is currently a nonprofit and does or plans to acquire a substantial amount of revenue through earned income, do you know if the income is related to your mission? If this is not the case, you risk needing to pay tax on it, or losing your 501c3 status.
- Do you need to develop a human resources manual?
- Do you have contracts with your employees, independent contractors, and other entities with financial relationships to your organization?
- Do you have a non-compete agreement with the appropriate parties?

If you answered yes to any of the above questions, it is time to find a lawyer who can advise your organization.

---

6 You can download a copy of the ICE 2007 Report Card at www.rootcause.org/social_enterprises/ice.html. Also look for the Social Innovation Forum's 2007 Report Card at www.rootcause.org/social_enterprises/stf.html.

RISK MITIGATION

? What are the risks that may limit the possibility of your business plan succeeding?

● What are you planning to do to minimize those risks?

While the previous sections should be developed as part of an iterative process, this component is almost always last. Developing a Risk Mitigation section allows you to examine the risks that may limit your business plan's chances for success, and describes how you will minimize those risks. It often includes a contingency plan addressing a risk that all organizations face: what will happen if the organization experiences less than the predicted success in bringing in revenue? In addition, you may want to identify one or two core elements of the business plan that must succeed if the Social Impact Model is to be successful.

Many organizations tend to resist writing a Risk Mitigation section because they believe that it makes their business plans look weaker. In reality, however, anticipating potential pitfalls is an important part of demonstrating the strength of your business plan. For example, TAP-IN,

Anticipating potential pitfalls is an important part of demonstrating the strength of your business plan.

a project of the American Health Initiative, worked with Root Cause to develop a plan for building a national volunteer network of retired health professionals to help ease staffing shortages at free clinics. The organization identified several potential barriers to success in the Risk Mitigation section of the plan. These included the difficulty of making retired health care professionals aware of volunteer opportunities like TAP-IN, and differing state licensing requirements that would pose challenges to placing volunteers across states.

By identifying these potential barriers up front, TAP-IN was able to build strategies for overcoming them into its business plan. For instance, TAP-IN began testing a variety of marketing strategies in phase one in order to find the best way to reach retired health care professionals. The organization also chose to build its model in North Carolina and Virginia, states that are both home to a large number of retired health care professionals and that have less strict licensing requirements. Phase two involved working with free clinic leadership, professional societies, and licensing boards at the state level to help support the easing of requirements, once a successful model was in place. TAP-IN's ability to plan for potential barriers helped to build confidence with potential funders and to make the implementation of its business plan a success.

The "Risk Mitigation" section of your business plan should clearly describe each of the risks you anticipate and the ways in which you intend to mitigate them. There is no need for a goal for this section.

CONCLUDING STEP 3

As you arrive at the end of step three, you should have drafts for all of the sections listed above and dedicate some time for the working group to review them. In step four, you will compile these sections with those you wrote in step two—and ensure that your business plan tells a coherent and compelling story that will help you raise the money you will need to capitalize your plan.

STEP 3 CHECKLIST

- ○ Business plan timeline
- ○ Phase one strategy goals
- ○ "Team and Governance" section
- ○ "Financial Sustainability" section
- ○ "Marketing" section
- ○ "Technology" section
- ○ "Public Policy" section
- ○ "Measurement" section
- ○ "Risk Mitigation" section
- ○ List of appendices to complete in step four
- ○ Preliminary approval of the above sections from the working group
- ○ Refinement of step two sections and business plan working group approval
- ○ Continue stakeholder and road show updates

STEP 4
FINALIZING YOUR BUSINESS PLAN & PUTTING IT INTO ACTION

GOAL: Compile the sections of your business plan into one document and add your appendices, write your executive summary, secure final approval of your business plan, and prepare for your road show.

HOW A BUSINESS PLAN FOR ENDURING SOCIAL IMPACT LINKS ANALYSIS TO STRATEGY TO ACTION

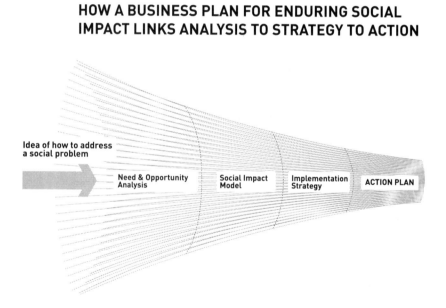

Idea of how to address a social problem

Need & Opportunity Analysis — Social Impact Model — Implementation Strategy — ACTION PLAN

As we enter step four, you can begin to see how a complete business plan for enduring social impact incorporates rigorous analysis, savvy strategic decision making, and a commitment to practicality, in order to better focus your organization's idea of where it wants to go and identify the best course of action. Through the "Need and Opportunity" section, the business plan opens with the big-picture analysis necessary for understanding your target social problem and the niche that your organization can fill. The "Social Impact Model" section articulates your organization's hypothesis about the best way to approach your target social problem, as well as the strategies that will enable you to test and measure that hypothesis. Following this section, the plan becomes progressively more concrete. The "Implementation Strategy," developed in step three, details how to put your social impact strategies to work, and how to build the capacity you will need in order to do so. Finally, an "Action Plan" section, created in step four, adds further detail to your implementation strategy, ensuring that you have a course of action to follow in the first phase of implementing your business plan.

As you complete and compile your business plan in step four, keep in mind that the narrative of the plan should follow this same trajectory—from analysis to strategy to action. Step four involves five tasks, starting with the development of your action plan:

1. DEVELOP AN ACTION PLAN FOR PHASE ONE

In step three, you established phase one goals for each section of your implementation strategy, and began identifying the activities necessary to complete those goals. An action plan for phase one allows you to describe in even greater detail the actions needed to meet those goals. This action plan will serve as your master to-do list to implement the plan.

The action plan is generally a spreadsheet that contains a series of worksheets. You will have one worksheet for each of the phase one strategy goals defined at the beginning of step three. You will also have an additional worksheet dedicated to your list of goals for organizational capacity building. Complete each worksheet by listing the goals you identified in step three and providing a complete list of the activities that will lead to achieving those goals. A good action plan also assigns a specific person who will be held accountable for each goal, along with the timeline for achieving each goal and activity.

A good action plan assigns a specific person who will be held accountable for each goal, along with a timeline for achieving each goal and activity.

For an example of an action plan, see Appendix D (page 63). This appendix shows one worksheet of the action plan for Project My Time, a nonprofit building an out-of-school time system for children in Washington, D.C. The worksheet represents the list of actions for one of the organization's social impact strategies, which focused on building a communications strategy.

2. COMPILE THE SECTIONS OF YOUR BUSINESS PLAN INTO ONE DOCUMENT AND ADD APPENDICES

Business plans are meant to tell a story of your organization's planned social impact that will get current and future stakeholders, including social impact investors, excited and make them want to be involved. With this in mind, compiling the business plan into one document requires making sure there is a logical flow between sections.

You will also need to add your appendices at this point. This section can be quite long, as you will likely have encountered many places in the writing of your business plan that required additional detail.

If possible, the complete draft should be reviewed and approved by the working group before you go on to write the executive summary.

3. WRITE AN EXECUTIVE SUMMARY

After completing a full draft of the business plan with which the working group is comfortable, you can write your executive summary. The executive summary should be a two-to-four page summary of the entire plan, focusing particularly on why now and why you; the amount of funding sought; and the impact you expect to have as a result of implementing your plan. This document will serve as a short description of your business plan to send to anyone interested in learning about the organization's future plans.

4. SEEK REVIEW AND APPROVAL

The preliminary work you did to develop an update schedule, along with a work plan and approval process, should facilitate this necessary part of finalizing your business plan. Following the approval schedules that you developed in step one, distribute the complete plan to the appropriate reviewers and remind them of the deadlines for approval.

5. PREPARE TO LAUNCH YOUR ROAD SHOW

While the business plan is in the final review process, it is time to capitalize on your preparations for the road show. Schedule any meetings with potential social impact investors that are not already on your calendar, so that the process of raising money for your plan can begin the moment your business plan receives final approval. Generally, the road show takes place through a series of gatherings and one-on-one meetings that present the business plan to funders and other stakeholders, with the goal of raising all of the resources necessary for phase one of your business plan as quickly as possible. Once you have secured those resources, your organization can focus 100 percent of its time on executing the plan.

CONCLUDING STEP 4

As you complete step four, you should have a complete and approved business plan in hand, and you should already be preparing for what comes next: capitalizing your plan and putting it to work.

STEP 4 CHECKLIST

- ○ "Action Plan" section
- ○ Complete business plan, including appendices
- ○ Executive summary
- ○ Final approval from the working group and other stakeholders
- ○ Final schedule of meetings with potential social impact investors to launch your road show

CONCLUSION

Business planning is undoubtedly an intensive process that can feel daunting at the outset. What makes it worthwhile? Business planning, when done well, transforms organizations, enabling them to achieve a level of social impact that was previously unimaginable.

Embarking on a business planning process will push your organization to think about both its long-term impact and the ways in which it allocates resources on a day-to-day basis. It will provide your organization with the opportunity to talk with social impact investors, board members, and other stakeholders in ways you never could before, while giving your organization renewed focus and a clear path forward. Moreover, the recent boom in the field of social entrepreneurship has further demonstrated the promise of approaching social problem solving with the strategic thinking that business planning makes possible. Our own experience has shown us that there is no better way to lead a successful organization and to pursue enduring social impact.

What makes it worthwhile? Business planning, when done well, transforms organizations, enabling them to achieve a level of social impact that was previously unimaginable.

We envision a world in which, much like in the private sector, organizations and social impact investors use one document to make decisions about investments and to track progress to determine whether they will continue to invest. In this scenario, business planning for enduring social impact directs capital in a logical and predictable manner—to the organizations that demonstrate the best performance and impact. Ultimately, we believe a world with more business planning has the potential to enable a wide variety of organizations and their social impact investors to work together to significantly accelerate solutions to today's most pressing social problems.

APPENDIX A: GLOSSARY

Action while Planning: Identifying and undertaking limited projects during the business planning process that an organization feels confident it can learn from, without limiting the direction of its business planning. Action while planning projects inform the business plan and allow the organization to begin testing implementation methods during the planning process.

Business Plan for Enduring Social Impact™: A business plan for enduring social impact applies the strategic rigor and financial savvy of a traditional private-sector business plan to social problem solving. It defines a course of action—generally spanning three to five years—that will guide an organization in generating another kind of profit: lasting social impact. The completed business plan should also serve as a sales document to aid in securing financial and in-kind resources, and in arranging partnerships.

Capitalization Plan: In the private sector, capitalization refers to raising a specified sum of money to fund business activities. In a business plan for enduring social impact, a capitalization plan identifies the total amount of philanthropic investment that an organization must acquire in order to implement its plan, in addition to outlining the steps for raising it.

Dashboard: A regular report (monthly, quarterly, yearly) on an organization's performance, as measured by its selected indicators. A dashboard is used by senior leadership to make course corrections, and it is often distributed internally to staff and board members to track progress.

Earned Income: Any revenue generated by a nonprofit by charging for a particular service or product in order to finance its mission.

Executive Coaching: One-on-one advice and insights on decision making, meeting management, skills assessment, and more for the leader of an organization, and sometimes for other members of the leadership team or board.

Feedback Loop: The systems that will ensure that an organization returns regularly to its operating model and social impact strategies in order to make course corrections based on the data generated by its organizational and program performance indicators and its social and economic impact indicators.

Financial Sustainability: The state of having a reliable, at times diversified, revenue mix that will allow an organization to predict its annual revenue and the sources of that revenue with reasonable certainty.

Gap Analysis: The process of identifying the work that has already been done for each section of the business plan through existing documents, interviews, and working group meeting(s) in order to determine how much additional work will be needed to develop each section of the business plan.

In-Kind Resources: Contributions of time, goods, or services to a nonprofit organization.

Low-Profit Market: A market that is not yet developed enough to provide the return on investment generally expected by traditional investors.

Market Failure: When the cost of a good or service is higher than the price that individuals are able or willing to pay, yet the social benefits from that good or service make its availability worthwhile for maintaining a healthy, productive society.

Mission: A description of an organization's purpose, including its target beneficiaries, the activities it conducts in order to address its target social problem, and the outcomes it expects to achieve.

Operating Model: An articulation of the way in which an organization's activities work together to carry out its mission.

Organizational and Program Performance Indicators: Units of measurement that allow an organization to assess its capacity and the outputs, or direct short-term results, of its work. These indicators also assess the organization's direct short-term results in accomplishing the goals set for its social impact strategies.

Patient Capital: Investments made by social impact investors in for-profit companies who are willing to accept below-market returns for an extended period of time in exchange for social impact.

Report Card: An annual public report of a subset of an organization's dashboard results, which allows social impact investors and other key stakeholders to monitor the organization's progress and social impact.

Road Show: A series of gatherings and one-on-one meetings that present the business plan to social impact investors and other stakeholders, with the goal of raising all of the resources necessary for phase one of the business plan.

Social and Economic Impact Indicators: Units of measurement that assess an organization's long-term progress toward meeting its vision of success, and ultimately determine whether the organization's hypothesis about its approach to addressing its target social problem is working.

Social Entrepreneurship: The practice of responding to market failures with transformative, financially sustainable innovations aimed at solving social problems.

Social Impact Investor: Anyone whose primary expectation in providing investment to fund an organization is measurable social impact, regardless of organizational structure, ego, or political agenda. Social impact investors may be foundations, corporations, government, or individuals.

Social Impact Model™: Articulates an organization's hypothesis about the best way to address a target social problem, as well as the actions necessary to test and measure that hypothesis, while working toward an enduring solution. It provides the framework that will guide all the work carried out by the organization, at least over the time frame of the business plan.

Social Impact Strategies: The major strategies identified in a business plan for enduring social impact, which will be implemented to further the organization's mission and strengthen its operating model, in order to progress toward achieving its vision of success.

Social Problem Definition: A concise description of an organization's target social problem, which begins to clarify the organization's niche within its field and is based on the need and opportunity analysis.

Vision of Success: A description of how the world will be different if an organization is ultimately successful in addressing its target social problem and a description of the organization's role in realizing that vision.

APPENDIX B: OUTLINE OF A BUSINESS PLAN FOR ENDURING SOCIAL IMPACT

I. Executive Summary

II. Need and Opportunity
    A. Overview of Social Problem
    B. Current Trends
    C. Root Causes
    D. Environmental Landscape
    E. Barriers
    F. Opportunity

III. Social Impact Model
    A. Overview of Organization
    B. Social Impact Model Diagram (including social problem
       definition, mission, indicators, and vision of success)
    C. Description of Operating Model
    D. Description of Social Impact Strategies

IV. Implementation Strategy
    A. Business Plan Timeline
    B. Phase One Strategy Goals
    C. Organizational Capacity Building
       1. Team and Governance
       2. Financial Sustainability
          a. Financial Projections
          b. Capitalization Strategy
       3. Marketing
          a. Brand
          b. Target Market
          c. Partnerships
       4. Technology
       5. Public Policy
       6. Performance and Social Impact Measurement
          a. Indicators and Targets
          b. Feedback Loop
       7. Risk Mitigation

V. Phase One Action Plan

VI. Appendix

rootCAUSE ⊚

APPENDIX C: SAMPLE WORK PLAN

	MONTHS						
	1	2	3	4	5	6	7
STEP 1: PLANNING TO PLAN							
Establish business plan working group and approval process	•						
Establish stakeholder update process	•						
Develop and agree upon work plan and approval process	•						
Begin planning road show	•						
Conduct preliminary meetings for gap analysis	•						
Develop and finalize gap analysis	•	•					
STEP 2: ARTICULATING A SOCIAL IMPACT MODEL							
Conduct need and opportunity analysis		•					
Develop social problem definition		•					
Define vision, preliminary social and economic impact indicators, and mission		•					
Conduct operating model analysis		•	•				
Develop social impact strategies			•				

	MONTHS						
	1	2	3	4	5	6	7
Define preliminary organizational and program performance indicators			•				
Draft "Need and Opportunity," "Operating Model," and "Social Impact Model" sections			•				
Obtain preliminary approval of all three of the above with the working group			•				
Begin stakeholder and road show updates			•				
STEP 3: DEVELOPING AN IMPLEMENTATION STRATEGY							
Establish business plan timeline				•			
Create phase one strategy goals				•			
Develop "Team and Governance" section				•	•	•	
Develop "Financial Sustainability" section				•	•	•	
Develop "Marketing" section				•	•		
Develop "Technology" section				•	•		
Develop "Public Policy" section				•	•		
Develop "Measurement" section				•	•		
Develop "Risk Mitigation" section						•	
Obtain preliminary approval of all written sections with the working group					•	•	
Continue stakeholder and road show updates						•	
STEP 4: FINALIZING YOUR BUSINESS PLAN AND PUTTING IT INTO ACTION							
Create action plan						•	
Compile business plan and add appendices						•	•
Write executive summary							•
Review and finalize business plan							•

APPENDIX D: PROJECT MY TIME PHASE ONE ACTION PLAN — COMMUNICATIONS SECTION

PHASE I

Goal: Communicate clear messages about the importance of out-of-school time to targeted audiences

	LEAD RESPONSIBILITY	INPUT/APPROVAL	AUG-06 (or before)	SEP-06	OCT-06	NOV-06	DEC-06	JAN-07	FEB-07	MAR-07	APR-07	MAY-07	JUN-07
A) ESTABLISH BRAND AND MESSAGES													
1) Review proposed new name, tagline, ad campaign			●										
2) Test brand and messages with tag			●										
3) Test brand and messages with youth and parents			●	●									
4) Participate in conference call with other Wallace cities to develop consistent, approachable language to describe initiative				●									
5) Convene key partners to approve new name, etc.			●										
6) Develop logo graphic tools				●									
7) Develop one-pager and FAQ with new brand				●									

PHASE I

B) DEVELOP COMMUNICATIONS AND OUTREACH TOOLS

	LEAD RESPONSIBILITY	INPUT/APPROVAL	AUG-06 (or before)	SEP-06	OCT-06	NOV-06	DEC-06	JAN-07	FEB-07	MAR-07	APR-07	MAY-07	JUN-07
1) Create a database of key contacts, coded by sector, for broad and targeted messaging													
a) Provide initial set of 200 contacts			•										
b) Research and add 500 contacts to database			•										
c) Acquire DCPS contact list			•										
d) Complete database			•	•	•	•	•	•	•	•	•	•	•
e) Manage database													
2) Establish quarterly publication of electronic newsletter													
a) Develop electronic format		•	•										
b) Draft content			•										
c) Disseminate first newsletter				•									
d) Ongoing development and quarterly dissemination							•	•	•	•	•	•	•
e) Draft precursor — update e-letter			•										
f) Distribute precursor — update e-letter			•										
3) Launch Web site													
a) Develop strategy for targeted audiences			•										
b) Determine appropriate use of partner sites		•	•										

PHASE I

	LEAD RESPONSIBILITY	INPUT/APPROVAL	AUG-06 (or before)	SEP-06	OCT-06	NOV-06	DEC-06	JAN-07	FEB-07	MAR-07	APR-07	MAY-07	JUN-07
B) DEVELOP COMMUNICATIONS AND OUTREACH TOOLS (continued)													
c) Develop structure and content			•	•									
d) Announce Web site at Lights On event					•								
e) Monitor Web site usage					•	•	•	•	•	•	•	•	•
4) Produce targeted outreach materials													
a) Develop targeted case statements for individual donors, funders, and businesses				•									
b) Produce and disseminate DVD								•					
c) Develop flyers and related materials for pilot parents and youth								•					
d) Develop materials for religious leaders in pilot neighborhoods							•						
e) Develop materials for ethnic and immigrant organizations							•						
f) Develop posters for pilot schools							•						
g) Develop materials for potential champions				•	•	•	•	•	•	•	•		

PHASE I

	LEAD RESPONSIBILITY	INPUT/APPROVAL	AUG-06 (or before)	SEP-06	OCT-06	NOV-06	DEC-06	JAN-07	FEB-07	MAR-07	APR-07	MAY-07	JUN-07
C) SECURE MEDIA COVERAGE FOR KEY EVENTS AND INITIATIVE													
1) Grant announcement													
a) Outreach to media for grant announcement				●									
b) Document all outlets' coverage of grant announcement				●									
2) Launch													
a) Prelaunch message development							●	●					
b) Prelauch media training							●	●					
3) Ongoing													
a) Produce electronic press packet				●									
b) Ongoing outreach to reporters				●	●	●	●	●	●	●	●	●	●
D) DESIGN PUBLIC EDUCATION CAMPAIGN (with implementation plan)													
1) Develop ads based on market research, general OST messaging and pilot program specifics					●	●							
2) Photograph youth at out-of-school time programs				●	●								
3) Review communications audit and revise based on focus groups research				●									
4) Create draft timeline of rollout based on progress and status of pilot				●	●								
5) Contract with radio and advertisers per timeline							●						
6) Build public service relationship with hip-hop radio station							●	●					

rootCAUSE ◉

PHASE I

	LEAD RESPONSIBILITY	INPUT/APPROVAL	AUG-06 (or before)	SEP-06	OCT-06	NOV-06	DEC-06	JAN-07	FEB-07	MAR-07	APR-07	MAY-07	JUN-07
D) DESIGN PUBLIC EDUCATION CAMPAIGN (continued)													
7) Build public service relationship with local cable company							•	•					
E) HOLD FALL "LIGHTS ON" EVENT in partnership with "Getting Connected," DCPS, business, and funding communities													
1) Secure venue				•									
2) Send out save-the-date notices				•									
3) Develop program				•									
4) Develop budget				•									
5) Hire event coordinator				•									
6) Hire caterer				•									
7) Secure youth performers				•									
8) Design invitations				•									
9) Send out invitations				•									
10) Invite media				•									
11) Identify business leader				•									
12) Invite CBOs to exhibit				•									
F) SUPPORT OTHER PROJECT MY TIME STRATEGIES													
1) Craft updates for political candidates (city leaders)			•										
2) Develop background materials and invitation to Advisory Council (city leaders)			•	•									
3) Develop update (or introduction) to DCPS administrators and teachers (pilot program)			•	•									
4) Support community outreach at pilot sites (pilot program)					•	•	•						
5) Support showcase events at pilot sites (pilot program)									•	•	•	•	•

rootCAUSE ⊚

APPENDIX E: BONNIE CLAC BUSINESS PLAN FOR GROWTH

The Bonnie CLAC Business plan was developed by Root Cause Senior Consultant Andrew Wolk with Root Cause Consultants Larry Chait, Abby Fung, and Whitney Robbins in partnership with Bonnie CLAC CEO Robert Chambers and the Bonnie CLAC working group: Mary Burnett, Allan Ferguson, Robert E. Field, Sr., Leo Hamill, Jr., Robert G. Hansen, David Reeves, Rick Sayles, and Liz Sundee.

Root Cause is grateful to Bonnie CLAC for their willingness to share this plan for the benefit of other organizations working to advance innovation for social impact.

Business Plan for Growth
2008–2012

Robert Chambers
President & Co-Founder

Lebanon, NH
www.bonnieclac.org

Prepared By

Advancing Innovation for Social Impact

CONTENTS

EXECUTIVE SUMMARY

Founded in 2001, Bonnie CLAC is the only nonprofit car organization in the country that uses a comprehensive program to help very low to moderate income people establish positive credit so they can purchase new, reliable, and fuel-efficient cars at affordable prices. The program saves a client over $10,000 over the five-year period of the loan while also achieving a positive impact on the client's work, life, and health all while contributing to a more sustainable environment. On average, the program reduces carbon emissions by 36 metric tons of CO_2 per person over the life of the car.[1]

Bonnie CLAC is headquartered in Lebanon, New Hampshire, and operates a central district office with five satellite locations around the state. Since inception, Bonnie CLAC has financed 930 new cars, served 827 people, and arranged for over $13 million in loans, with a default rate of only 4%.[2] Bonnie CLAC has already saved alumni of the program over $1.8 million and will save them over $9 million over the course of their loans.

Bonnie CLAC guides the very low to moderate income consumer through the car-buying process from start to finish. It provides counseling, teaches financial literacy classes, and guarantees car loans at wholesale interest rates to consumers who would not otherwise qualify for them to finance brand-new Honda Civics, Toyota Corollas, and other cars that suit the clients' needs. Bonnie CLAC instituted the very first, and to-date only, lending relationship between a financial institution and a nonprofit organization to provide wholesale financing rates to very low to moderate income consumers.[3] In just six years, Bonnie CLAC has established itself as the premiere nonprofit car program in the country.[4]

Bonnie CLAC has now begun work on expanding throughout New England leading toward nationwide expansion. Bonnie CLAC's goal is

---

1 http://www.stopglobalwarming.org/carboncalculator.asp?c=2;
   Assumes 10-year life span
2 www.bonnieclac.org and from the Bonnie CLAC QuickBase database.
3 From Bonnie CLAC.
4 See awards and prizes listed at http://www.bonnieclac.org/about/
   Program outcomes results are also available via a third-party evaluation performed by
   Sally Ward and Sarah Savage. "Bonnie CLAC Interview Analysis." Carsey Institute,
   University of New Hampshire, Fall 2007.

to make its services available to the tens of millions of very low to moderate income consumers across the United States who are still suffering from the consequences of expensive, unreliable automobiles. Over the next five years, Bonnie CLAC will establish 25 new districts, and expand its impact in the following ways:

	PHASE I		PHASE II		
	2008	2009	2010	2011	2012
Annual Clients Served	280	474	963	1,875	3,485
Annual Client Savings	$560,000	$948,000	$1.9mm	$3.8mm	$7.0mm
Annual Loans Guaranteed	$4.2mm	$7.1mm	$14.4mm	$28.1mm	$52.3mm
CO_2 Reduction (metric tons)	1,016	2,736	6,231	13,034	25,681

In order to accomplish this, Bonnie CLAC is seeking $2.7 million to support the first phase of the business plan expansion through 2008.

Need & Opportunity

According to the 2005 American Community Survey of the US Census Bureau, there are 42.5 million very low to moderate income households in the United States with incomes not exceeding $34,999[5] making up approximately 17% of the total US population. In 2005, they spent approximately $85 billion on used cars, comprising 24% of the $353 billion used car market.[6]

When making car purchases, very low to moderate income households are faced with limited options. The lack of reliable cars at decent financing terms for very low to moderate income households forces them to purchase expensive, unreliable cars again and again, which result in dire work and credit consequences, poor health conditions, and negative environmental impacts.[7,8,9] According to an Aspen Institute re-

5 US Census Bureau. "2005 American Community Survey." http://factfinder.census.gov/servlet/DatasetMainPageServlet?_program=ACS&_submenuId=&_lang=en&_ts=

6 Automotive News Data Center, CNW Marketing/Research and ADESA Analytical Services. 42.5 million very low to moderate income households divided by four (a quarter of households purchase cars each year) = 10.6 million very low to moderate income households * $7,998 (average price of used car) = $85 billion.

7 Goldberg, Heidi (Nov 2001). "State and County Supported Car Ownership Programs Can Help Very low-Income Families Secure and Keep Jobs." Center on Budget and Policy Priorities. http://www.nedlc.org/center/Jump_start.pdf

8 Blumenberg, Evelyn (2002). "On the Way to Work: Welfare Participants and Barriers to Employment," Economic Development Quarterly, 16(4): 314-325. http://www.nedlc.org/center/copc/otherresources/On_the_way_to_work.pdf

9 Raphael, Steven and Lorien Rice, "Car Ownership, Employment, and Earnings," National Science Foundation, SBR-9709197 and the Joint Center for Poverty Research. http://www.jcpr.org/wpfiles/RaphaelSG2000.pdf?CFID=7752296&CFTOKEN=35709093

port, 90% of very low to moderate income households purchase vehicles that are "bad, vastly overpriced, and wildly over financed"[10] while the remaining 10% do not even own a car.[11]

In the 21st century, owning a car has become more important than ever.[12] Job locations have shifted away from urban areas so that three-quarters of jobs are located in the suburbs,[13] while many very low to moderate income Americans live in metropolitan or rural areas without benefit of public transportation.[14] Congresswoman Gwendolynne S. Moore (D-WI), a member of the Financial Services and Small Business Committee in the US House of Representatives, said, "For many low-income families, getting to a job can be even harder than getting hired in the first place. Entry-level jobs of low-income workers are increasingly found in the far-away plants, warehouses, strip malls, and office parks of suburbia."[15]

Over the past six years, Bonnie CLAC has developed and refined a comprehensive car purchase program to help very low to moderate income consumers successfully obtain new, reliable, and fuel-efficient cars at affordable prices. Bonnie CLAC's program is differentiated and successful for the following five reasons:

1. A focus on new cars

2. Guaranteed financing at wholesale interest rates through unique partnerships with financial institutions (currently 6.84%)

3. Assistance in establishing (or re-establishing) a positive credit rating

4. Comprehensive support of the car-buying process from beginning to end

5. Promotion of fuel-efficient vehicles

---

10 Sutton, Remar (Apr 2007). "Car Financing for Very Low and Moderate Income Consumers." The Consumer Task Force for Automotive Issues and the Aspen Institute: 14.
11 Blumenberg, Evelyn. "Transportation and Very low Income Households." http://www.brookings.edu/es/events/20051205_Blumenberg.ppt#16
12 (In 2000, fewer than 5% of workers took public transportation to work, while nearly 88% commuted by car.)
   Waller, Margy (Dec 2005). "High Cost or High Opportunity Cost? Transportation and Family Economic Success." The Brookings Institution Policy Brief. http://www.brookings.edu/es/research/projects/wrb/publications/pb/pb35.htm
13 Waller: 3.
14 Waller: 3.
15 Moore, Gwendolynne S. (May 2005). "Press Release for US House of Representatives." http://www.house.gov/list/press/wi04_moore/pr120505.html

The Bonnie CLAC Operating Model

Bonnie CLAC's proven operating model utilizes a seven-step process. The seven steps are:

1. Recruiting

2. Screening

3. One-on-One Counseling or FastTrack

4. Vehicle Selection

5. Financing

6. Delivery of a New Car

7. Alumni Support

Throughout the process, Bonnie CLAC Client Consultants meet regularly with clients to provide step-by-step guidance. This one-on-one relationship, and the trust that results from this close bond, makes Bonnie CLAC unique and effective in working with this often-challenging population. Other personnel involved in the process include an Intake Manager who screens calls, a Financial Fitness Instructor who teaches financial literacy classes, a BRIDGE Manager who provides transitional loaner cars to clients who need them while they complete the program, and a Delivery Manager who supports car selection, completes the necessary financing paperwork and manages the delivery of the new car upon program completion. Bonnie CLAC's comprehensive process has enabled it to improve the lives of the New Hampshire residents it has served[16] while maintaining a loan default rate of only four percent.[17]

---

16 Ward, Sally and Sarah Savage. "Bonnie CLAC Interview Analysis." Carsey Institute, University of New Hampshire, Fall 2007.
17 www.bonnieclac.org

Bonnie CLAC Strategies for Sustainability, Growth, & Impact

Over the next five years, Bonnie CLAC is committed to carrying out a five-pronged strategy that will enable it to reach a greater percentage of the 42.5 million very low to moderate income households in the United States. With stronger systems and infrastructure in place, Bonnie CLAC will be ready to have significant and enduring impact in making the ownership of new cars affordable to everyone in the targeted population through guaranteed low interest loans. Bonnie CLAC's five-pronged growth strategy is:

1. Establish districts that will become profitable and contribute financially toward national operations

2. Develop the infrastructure needed to support national expansion

3. Implement a rigorous measurement & quality program

4. Develop state and national partnerships

5. Support public policies

Business Plan Timeline

Bonnie CLAC will use a phased approach to implement its business plan, with the following goals defined for each phase:

PHASE I: Piloting new districts in select New England states and building national support systems Jan 2008–Dec 2009 (2 Years)	• Launch four new districts • Solidify national leadership team and operations • Build a robust measurement and quality system • Establish initial state and national partnerships • Begin public policy work
PHASE II: Testing growth of districts nationwide Jan 2010–Dec 2011 (2 Years)	• Make necessary course corrections for district model • Select sites and test district model beyond New England

PHASE III: ▪ Scale Bonnie CLAC operations nationwide

Scaling
Nationwide

2012 (1+ Years)

Financial Sustainability

The foundation of Bonnie CLAC's financial strategy is to operate lean districts that will become profitable by efficiently capturing local market share and successfully converting prospects to clients. Each client contributes $1,065 in program fees, driving each new district to profitability in Year 3 of operations. Bonnie CLAC has made the conscious decision not to raise client fees, as volume alone can make this model sustainable over time. Bonnie CLAC will focus on partnerships with banks, automobile manufacturers and rental car companies which could also increase sustainability.

Below is a summary of the financials and investment required for the entire span of the business plan. Bonnie CLAC has already raised $1.2 million toward national expansion. Bonnie CLAC is now seeking an additional $2.7 million in Phase I and an additional $9.6 million in Phase II for a total capitalization of approximately $12.3 million over the next five years. Approximately $4.3 million of the $12.3 million Bonnie CLAC is raising will go toward launching 25 new district offices.

	PHASE I: 2008-2009	PHASE II: 2010-2012
Total Expenses	$5,290,855	$20,429,965
Total Earned Revenues	$1,521,731	$10,743,530
Total Committed Funds Raised to Date	$1,060,500	$125,000
Total Capitalization Required	$2,708,624	$9,561,435

Measuring Performance and Impact

The Carsey Institute at the University of New Hampshire recently performed Bonnie CLAC's first third-party evaluation of program outcomes, with many outstanding results.[18] The preliminary data on 48 responses received and coded to date show the following:

---

18 Ward, Sally and Sarah Savage. "Bonnie CLAC Interview Analysis." Carsey Institute, University of New Hampshire, Fall 2007.

- Although relatively few respondents have actually changed their jobs or earnings (10% and 17% respectively), getting to their jobs and doing so punctually have improved (48% and 38%).

- The majority of respondents report that their overall financial situation has improved (69%), and almost half are better able to pay their bills. Respondents to date report spending less on gas (39%), insurance (27%), repairs (75%), and interest rates (42%). In an independent analysis, the Root Cause Institute calculated that the average Bonnie CLAC client saves over $2,000 a year, or over $10,000 over the five-year lifespan of the average Bonnie CLAC car loan.[19]

- The majority of respondents report being better able to provide transportation for family members (56%), and many report improved ability to attend children's activities (33%). Almost half attend more community events, and three-quarters are in a better position to shop and run errands.

- Over half are better able to make health and dental appointments, and over a third have greater options for purchasing food and for health care.

In the future, Bonnie CLAC will measure the impact of its work in the following three ways:

1. **Implement indicators:** Bonnie CLAC will assess the progress and impact of its organization on an ongoing basis by implementing organizational and program-performance indicators and social impact indicators. The social impact indicators are divided into three categories to measure economic, health/lifestyle, and environmental impact.

2. **Implement measurement tools and tracking system:** Bonnie CLAC will build measurement tools and an organization-wide tracking system that enables organizational-health and program-performance indicators to be automatically captured as part of Bonnie CLAC's daily operations. Social and economic indicators will be collected via intake interviews, as well as from surveys and/or interviews of alumni upon graduation, and 6, 12, and 18 months later.

---

19 See Table C on page 89: Annual Cost of Bonnie CLAC New Cars vs. Buy-Here, Pay-Here Used Cars in Bonnie CLAC Business Plan.

3. **Implement feedback and self-evaluation:** Staff members will analyze indicators on a regular basis to determine whether Bonnie CLAC is meeting set goals and metrics. If it is not, appropriate action steps will be taken to remedy the problem(s).

In addition, Bonnie CLAC will hire a long-term third-party evaluator to track the longitudinal impact of its work. These efforts will further validate the credibility of Bonnie CLAC's program and enable the organization to attract government and other funding support in future years.

In five years, Bonnie CLAC will provide nationwide access to credit at affordable interest rates and educational opportunities, so that very low to moderate income individuals may obtain reliable and affordable cars. Since its founding, Bonnie CLAC will have served 8,117 clients throughout the United States, guaranteed nearly $121.8 million in loans, and saved its clients more than $16.2 million. In addition, it will have reduced carbon dioxide emissions by more than 52,000 metric tons, the equivalent of taking 17,060 passenger cars off the roads for a year or preserving 646 acres of forest from deforestation.[20]

I. NEED & OPPORTUNITY

Need

A. Social Problem

Very low to moderate income households are faced with limited options when making car purchases, resulting in dire work and credit consequences, poor health conditions, and negative environmental impacts.[21,22,23] According to an Aspen Institute report, 90% of very low to moderate income households purchase vehicles that are "bad, vastly overpriced, and wildly over financed"[24] while the remaining 10% do not even own a car.[25]

20 U.S. Climate Technology Corporation Gateway (http://www.usctcgateway.net/tool/)
21 Goldberg, Heidi (Nov 2001). "State and County Supported Car Ownership Programs Can Help Very low-Income Families Secure and Keep Jobs." Center on Budget and Policy Priorities. http://www.nedlc.org/center/Jump_start.pdf
22 Blumenberg, Evelyn (2002). "On the Way to Work: Welfare Participants and Barriers to Employment," Economic Development Quarterly, 16(4): 314-325. http://www.nedlc.org/center/copc/otherresources/On_the_way_to_work.pdf
23 Raphael, Steven and Lorien Rice, "Car Ownership, Employment, and Earnings," National Science Foundation, SBR-9709197 and the Joint Center for Poverty Research. http://www.jcpr.org/wpfiles/RaphaelSG2000.pdf?CFID=7752296&CFTOKEN=35709093
24 Sutton, Remar (Apr 2007). "Car Financing for Very low and Moderate Income Consumers." The Consumer Task Force for Automotive Issues and the Aspen Institute: 14.
25 Blumenberg, Evelyn. "Transportation and Very low Income Households." http://www.brookings.edu/es/events/20051205_Blumenberg.ppt#16

While this population has limited access to a reliable car, having a reliable car has become more important than ever.[26] In the 21st century, three-quarters of jobs are located in the suburbs,[27] while many very low to moderate income Americans live in metropolitan or rural areas without benefit of public transportation.[28] Congresswoman Gwendolynne S. Moore (D-WI), a member of the Financial Services and Small Business Committee in the US House of Representatives, said, "For many low-income families, getting to a job can be even harder than getting hired in the first place. Entry-level jobs of low-income workers are increasingly found in the faraway plants, warehouses, strip malls, and office parks of suburbia."[29]

The US Department of Housing and Urban Development (HUD) defines very low to moderate income households as those households earning an annual income not exceeding 80% of an area's median income (AMI). Area median incomes vary by county and state, but the US median household income in 2005 was $46,242.[30] Therefore, the upper limit for very low to moderate income households of four in the US is an annual income not exceeding $36,994 (or 80% of $46,242).[31] According to the 2005 American Community Survey of the US Census Bureau, there are 42.5 million very low to moderate income households in the United States with incomes not exceeding $34,999,[32] making up approximately 17% of the total US population. In 2005, they spent approximately $85 billion on used cars, comprising 24% of the $353 billion used car market.[33] This means a significant number of US households are stuck with transportation options that seriously limit their ability to

---

26 (In 2000, fewer than 5% of workers took public transportation to work, while nearly 88% commuted by car.) Waller, Margy (Dec 2005). "High Cost or High Opportunity Cost? Transportation and Family Economic Success." The Brookings Institution Policy Brief. http://www.brookings.edu/es/research/projects/wrb/publications/pb/pb35.htm
27 Waller: 3.
28 Waller: 3.
29 Moore, Gwendolynne S. (May 2005). "Press Release for US House of Representatives." http://www.house.gov/list/press/wi04_moore/pr120505.html
30 US Census Bureau. "2005 American Community Survey." http://factfinder.census.gov/servlet/DatasetMainPageServlet?_program=ACS&_submenuId=&_lang=en&_ts=
31 Very low income is defined by the federal government as 30% of an area's median income (AMI), low income is defined as 50% of AMI, and moderate income is defined as 80% of AMI. http://www.hud.gov/offices/cpd/systems/census/lowmod/index.cfm Based on the US median household income from the 2005 Census, the very low income upper limit is $13,873; the low income upper limit is $23,121; and the moderate income upper limit is $36,994. To calculate income limits for families larger or smaller than four, increase the limit by 8% for each person above four or reduce it by 10% for each person below four. http://www.hud.gov/offices/cpd/systems/census/lowmod/calculation.cfm
32 US Census Bureau. "2005 American Community Survey." http://factfinder.census.gov/servlet/DatasetMainPageServlet?_program=ACS&_submenuId=&_lang=en&_ts=
33 Automotive News Data Center, CNW Marketing/Research and ADESA Analytical Services. 42.5 million very low to moderate income households divided by four (a quarter of households purchase cars each year) = 10.6 million very low to moderate income households * $7,998 (average price of used car) = $85 billion.

lead productive and healthy lives and contribute to high levels of carbon emissions.

B. Root Cause

Very low to moderate income households have limited options when making car purchases because they lack the knowledge, resources, negotiating skills, and consumer credit scores necessary to access affordable interest rates. For the most part, remedies to correct these problems—in the form of education, advice, and financing—are unavailable to very low to moderate income consumers.

In desperation, consumers in this income category turn to "buy-here, pay-here" used car dealers, who do not require credit checks, a good credit history, or a minimum credit score. Unfortunately, these used car dealerships often take advantage of their desperate clientele by inflicting high prices, high interest rates, and large down payments. Ralph Nader calls these practices "consumer oppression…and servitude."[34] In addition to the onerous financial burden, used cars break down much more frequently, often require more expensive repairs, consume larger amounts of gasoline, release more carbon emissions, and carry only slightly lower insurance costs than newer, more fuel-efficient cars. It is not unusual for very low to moderate income households to have used car loan obligations outstanding even after their cars have broken down and can no longer function as transportation.[35]

The lack of reliable cars at decent financing terms for very low to moderate income households forces them to purchase expensive, unreliable cars again and again, which contribute to a downward spiral of poverty. In *The Working Poor: Invisible in America*, David K. Shipler, a Pulitzer Prize winning New York Times reporter and university lecturer, writes, "A run-down apartment can exacerbate a child's asthma, which leads to a call for an ambulance, which generates a medical bill that cannot be paid, which ruins a credit record, which hikes the interest rate on an auto loan, which forces the purchase of an unreliable used car, which jeopardizes a mother's punctuality at work, which limits her promotions and earning capacity, which confines her to poor housing."[36]

34 Meredith, Robin. "Auto Dealer Has an Offer for Drivers with Bad Credit, but There's a Catch." New York Times. 30 Aug. 1999.
35 Compiled from Bonnie CLAC Client Consultants anecdotes and Meredith, Robin. "Auto Dealer Has an Offer for Drivers with Bad Credit, but There's a Catch." New York Times. 30 Aug 1999.
36 Lacayo, Richard. "Take This Job and Starve." Time. 9 Feb. 2004: http://www.time.com/time/magazine/article/0,9171,588868,00.html. See also *The Working Poor: Invisible in America* by David K. Shipler (New York: Vintage Books, 2005).

Environmental Landscape
C. The For-Profit Car Market

Figure A: 2005 US Car Market Sales in Units

The American car market is a $777 billion annual business. In 2005, 17.0 million new cars were sold in the United States, totaling $424 billion and making up 28% of the units sold (see Figure A).[37] Most very low to moderate income consumers do not even consider going to new car dealerships to purchase a new car because they don't think they'll be able to afford it.

Instead, they go to one of more than 100,000 used car dealerships in the United States.[38] In 2005 used car dealerships sold 44.1 million cars, totaling $353 billion and making up 72% of the units sold.[39]

"Buy-here, pay-here" dealerships charge substantial down payments for used cars that have short lifespans. In addition, they exercise predatory, though legal, lending practices, charging up to 25% interest on monthly car payments.[40] While used car dealers may tell consumers that they "'work with many different banks and…will give you the best interest [rate] for which you qualify'…this is serious misinformation," says Robert Chambers, co-founder of Bonnie CLAC. "The finance manager will choose the bank that pays the dealership the most profit."[41]

---

37 Automotive News Data Center, CNW Marketing/Research, and ADESA Analytical Services.
38 Sutton: 16.
39 Automotive News Data Center, CNW Marketing/Research, and ADESA Analytical Services.
40 "Buy Here, Pay Here Industry Benchmarks," prepared for the National Alliance of Buy Here, Pay Here Dealers, Shilson, Goldberg, Cheung and Associates, L.L.P., http://www.kenshilson.com
41 Vogel, John H. Jr. (Mar 2005). "Bonnie CLAC Case Study." Tuck School of Business at Dartmouth: 2-3.

In addition to profit on a sale, when they originate a loan, car dealers make both a flat fee and a premium tied to any markup on the interest rate.[42] Therefore, it is not unusual for car dealers to mark up the loan three to five percentage points above the actual rate of the loan in order to increase their profit margins.[43] Using these tactics, used car dealerships can make as much as $3,500 gross profit on the sale of a single used car.[44]

According to the Consumer Federation of America, "Consumers who finance at the dealership are shown a document with a rate, but they are never told that the rate has been arbitrarily marked up by the dealer and that they could do better, given their creditworthiness. Similar practices in home mortgage lending have been outlawed."[45]

D. The Nonprofit Car Market

In recent years, increased social awareness of the many unfair and unethical business practices of the for-profit car market has led to the creation and growth of a nonprofit car market. The National Economic Development and Law Center's Low-Income Car Ownership (LICO) Clearinghouse has identified 151 LICO Programs in active operation around the country.[46] One hundred and eight organizations responded to a survey administered by the Center in Summer 2006, which allowed the Center to identify some key characteristics of the nonprofit car market (see Table A).[47] While substantial growth has taken place in the number of nonprofit car programs in the past few years, cars obtained through these programs still make up less than 1% of the overall US car market.

---

42 Ibid.
43 Consumer Federation of America (Jan 2004) "The Hidden Markup of Auto Loans," www.consumerfed.org: 6.
44 Interview with Robert Chambers.
45 Consumer Federation of America: 5.
46 Lohrentz, Tim (Jun 2007). "Low-Income Car Ownership Programs—2006 Survey." National Economic Development & Law Center for the Annie E. Casey Foundation: 4. http://www.opportunitycars.com/Articles/LICOreport.pdf
47 Lohrentz: 4 (Function): 6 (Size & Reach)

Table A: Characteristics of US Low-Income Car Ownership Programs

LOW-INCOME CAR OWNERSHIP PROGRAMS IN THE UNITED STATES

Size Most programs are small, regionally focused, and new.

- Median annual budget—$126,000
- 39% have one staff person or less
- Median number of cars distributed per year—35
- Median start year—2000

Reach LICO organizations are spread throughout the United States.

- Organizations exist in 33 of 50 states.
- Highest number in New York, Minnesota, Pennsylvania, and Wisconsin

Function Most serve as financiers or acquirers/distributors.

- 46% of all nonprofit car organizations finance cars and 44% acquire and distribute them.
- The remaining 10% consists of Individual Development Account (IDA) matched savings programs.[48]

E. The Nonprofit Car Market Landscape

The nonprofit car market consists of nonprofit organizations that help disadvantaged consumers obtain used or new cars. The nonprofit used car market can be divided further into organizations with functional expertise in financing as opposed to those with expertise in acquisition and distribution. Table B presents a profile of three types of organizations active in the nonprofit car market: 1) a nonprofit used car financier, 2) a nonprofit used car acquirer & distributor, and 3) a nonprofit new car financier and counselor.

---

48 In recent years, Individual Development Accounts (IDAs) have become popular as an asset-building strategy for low-income individuals. IDAs are income-eligible savings accounts that are matched anywhere from a 1:1 to a 4:1 ratio from a combination of private and public sources.

Table B: Nonprofit Car Market Competitive Landscape

Criteria	Ways to Work	Good News Garage	Bonnie CLAC
Type of Organization	Nonprofit Used Cars	Nonprofit Used Cars	Nonprofit New Cars
Relationship to Vehicle	Financier	Acquirer & Distributor	Financier & Full-Service Counselor
Type of Cars	Used Cars	Donated, used cars	New Toyota Corollas, Honda Civics, & other client-appropriate vehicles
Financing Mechanism	Foundations and banks provide program-related investment into a loan pool fund	None; cars are either given away or sold for a small fee	Partners with financial institutions that provide loans
Number of Offices	45 in 25 states	3 in New England	6 in NH
Year Founded	1984	1996	2001
HQ	Milwaukee, WI	Burlington, VT	Lebanon, NH

1. Nonprofit Used Car Market

Cars obtained through nonprofit used car organizations number approximately 24,000 a year.[49] Some organizations focus strictly on financing used cars, while others acquire used cars, fix them up, and then distribute them to the needy.

Ways to Work affiliate offices make up roughly 70% of the nonprofit financiers.[50] Ways to Work was founded in 1984 by the McKnight Foundation in Minnesota. Since inception, Ways to Work has financed over 10,000 loans exceeding $21 million.[51] Today, it operates 45 offices in 25 states and is a federally-certified Community Development Financial Institution (CDFI) headquartered in Milwaukee, Wisconsin. Ways to Work partners with the Alliance for Children and Families to establish its offices within new Alliance sites. At the local level, the program is administered by a loan officer, who receives technical assistance and oversight from

---

49 Sutton: 16.
50 Lohrentz: 12.
51 http://www.waystowork.com/pages/p_hstry-milestns.html

Ways to Work.[52] Ways to Work partners with foundations and banks to provide a loan pool fund from which to finance modestly-priced used vehicles for needy families.[53] However, Ways to Work does not assist its loan recipients with other steps of the car purchase process.

Good News Garage is a prime example of an acquirer and distributor. Good News Garage began in Burlington, Vermont, in 1996 as a community garage "where even poor people could buy a car that would be in working condition and safe to drive."[54] Good News Garage solicits donated cars, fixes them up, and then gives them away to recipients of Temporary Assistance to Needy Families (TANF) or sells them for a small fee to low-income applicants sponsored by local church and civic groups. Since its founding in 1996, Good News Garage has helped over 2,000 individuals and families.[55] Today, Good News Garage, in partnership with Lutheran Social Services of New England, operates three community garages in the New England region.

2. Nonprofit New Car Market

Founded in 2001, Bonnie CLAC is the only nonprofit car organization that utilizes a comprehensive program to help very low to moderate income consumers establish positive credit ratings so they can purchase new, reliable, and fuel-efficient cars at affordable prices. Bonnie CLAC guides the very low to moderate income consumer through the car-buying process from start to finish. It provides counseling, teaches financial literacy classes, and guarantees car loans at wholesale interest rates to consumers who would not otherwise qualify for them to finance brand-new Honda Civics, Toyota Corollas, and other cars that suit the clients' needs. Bonnie CLAC instituted the very first, and to-date, only, lending relationship between a bank and a nonprofit organization in order to provide wholesale financing rates to very low to moderate income consumers.[56]

Bonnie CLAC is headquartered in Lebanon, New Hampshire, and operates in six locations around the state. Since inception, Bonnie CLAC has financed 930 new cars, served 827 people, and arranged for over $13 million in automobile loans with a default rate of only 4%.[57]

---

52 http://waystowork.org/pages/p_business-model.html
53 2006 Evaluation of the national Ways to Work program from www.waystowork.org
54 http://www.goodnewsgarage.org/about_us/
55 Primack, Phil. (Winter 2006). "Want to Give Away That Old Jalopy? Here's Good News." CommonWealth: 15. http://www.goodnewsgarage.org/about_us/media_coverage/
56 From Bonnie CLAC.
57 www.bonnieclac.org and from Bonnie CLAC QuickBase database.

Opportunity

Over the past six years, Bonnie CLAC has developed and refined a comprehensive car purchase program to help very low to moderate income consumers successfully obtain new, reliable, and fuel-efficient cars at affordable prices. For a one-time cost of approximately $865 per client,[58] Bonnie CLAC can potentially save that client more than $10,000 over the course of his or her five-year loan payment period (see Table C below) while bringing about many positive, long-term social, economic and environmental impacts (discussed in greater detail in Section IX of this business plan).

In addition to a successful program model, Bonnie CLAC has also developed a successful operational model. A local Bonnie CLAC district office can be financially profitable within a few years after its launch and help contribute to the expenses of running a national office. After proven success in New Hampshire, Bonnie CLAC is ready to scale this program nationwide. Bonnie CLAC has developed this business plan into a roadmap for remedying the reliable transportation problem for millions of very low to moderate income individuals, in order to help them lead more productive and healthy lives.

Bonnie CLAC's program is differentiated and successful for the following five reasons: 1) a focus on new cars, 2) guaranteed financing at wholesale interest rates, 3) assistance in establishing (or re-establishing) a positive credit rating, 4) comprehensive support of the car-buying process from beginning to end, and 5) promotion of fuel-efficient vehicles.

1. A Focus on New Cars

New cars break the cycle of poverty by requiring fewer repairs, providing greater safety and reliability, and creating economic self-sufficiency for the owner. According to Table C below, a new car can save a Bonnie CLAC client over $2,000 each year, compared to a used car from a "buy-here, pay-here" dealership. For a household earning $20,000 a year, this represents 10% of their total salary that could be spent on other critical needs.

---

58 From Bonnie CLAC.

Table C: Annual Cost of Bonnie CLAC New Car vs. "Buy-Here, Pay-Here" Used Cars

	Bonnie CLAC (nonprofit new cars)	Buy here, pay here dealerships (for-profit used cars)
Default Rate	4% [1]	39% [2]
Interest Rate	6.8% [1]	24.5% [2]
Payment Lifespan	5 [3]	3 [2]
Down payment annualized for lifespan	$0 [1]	$837/3= $279 [2]
Enrollment fee annualized for lifespan [1]	$65/5=13	$0
Car fee annualized for lifespan [1]	$800/5=$160	$0
Annual Payments (Principal + Interest)	$285 * 12 = $3,420 [1]	$74 * 52 = $3,848 [2]
Annual Insurance [4]	$1,140	$850
Annual Maintenance & Repairs [4]	$160	$540
Annual Gas	$1,449[5]	$1,751 [6]
Total Annual Costs	**$6,342**	**$7,268**
Residual value annualized for lifespan	$5,555/5 = $1,111 [7]	$0
Total Annual Costs minus residual value	**$5,231**	**$7,268**
Annual Difference		**$2,037**

[1] Provided by Bonnie CLAC

[2] "Buy Here, Pay Here Industry Benchmarks," prepared for the National Alliance of Buy Here, Pay Here Dealers, Shilson, Goldberg, Cheung and Associates, L.L.P; http://www.kenshilson.com

[3] A Bonnie CLAC car takes five years to pay off.

[4] http://www.edmunds.com/advice/buying/articles/47079/article.html

[5] Annual fuel cost for 2007 Toyota Corolla, www.fueleconomy.gov based on 45% highway driving, 55% city driving, 15,000 miles/year and $2.80 per gallon.

[6] Annual fuel cost for 1998 Subaru Legacy, www.fueleconomy.gov based on 45% highway driving, 55% city driving, 15,000 miles/year and $2.80 per gallon.

[7] Kelley Blue Book trade-in value, 2002 Toyota Corolla, 75k miles, good condition

2. Financing Partnerships at Wholesale Interest Rates

By serving as a financing guarantor, Bonnie CLAC makes car loans available to very low to moderate income individuals at lower rates than they could access as individuals. Both for-profit used car dealerships and other nonprofit car organizations tend to provide financing at higher interest rates than Bonnie CLAC because used cars have higher interest rates than new cars. Because banks are concerned about the value of loan collateral, they want to be paid a significant premium for older cars.[59] Therefore, the older

---

59 Vogel: 4.

the car, the higher the interest rate the bank will charge for car loan financing. While Bonnie CLAC provides wholesale interest rates for new automobiles at 6.8%, used car interest rates can start at 9% and run as high as 25% for "buy-here, pay-here" used car dealerships.[60,61]

In addition, Bonnie CLAC is able to offer consistently low interest rates regardless of the number of transactions conducted annually, because it does not rely on loan funds to provide financing, which can limit the number of transactions nonprofit car financiers are able to conduct.

3. Credit Rating Rehabilitation

Bonnie CLAC not only helps very low to moderate income individuals obtain financing to purchase cars, but it also helps them repair their credit and establish (or re-establish) a positive credit rating. Based on a client's individual credit history and ability to make payments, a Client Consultant will perform a one-on-one credit analysis and determine the most appropriate credit counseling for that client. Client Consultants will give clients "assignments" toward credit repair and (re)establishment of a positive payment history. Bonnie CLAC helps its clients rehabilitate their credit ratings and establish positive financial habits and ways of thinking that will last well beyond the transaction of a car purchase.

4. Comprehensive Car Buying Support from Soup to Nuts

Many very low to moderate income households also lack the critical knowledge, resources, and negotiating skills needed to obtain good cars at affordable prices. Bonnie CLAC provides one-on-one counseling, financial literacy education, access to a temporary car through a BRIDGE program, guidance in making car purchase decisions, and assistance in executing car purchase processes. By guiding its clients step by step through the car buying process, and maintaining regular contact throughout the duration of the car loan to provide further troubleshooting and guidance as necessary, Bonnie CLAC has been able to maintain an exceptionally low default rate of 4%, compared to 15% for Ways to Work, and up to 40% for "buy-here, pay-here" used car dealerships.[62,63,64]

---

60 Meredith, Robin.

61 Vogel: 4.

62 "Enterprising Ideas: Lending a Hand." NOW. Host David Brancaccio. Public Broadcasting System. 22 June 2007. http://www.pbs.org/now/transcript/325.html

63 From Ways to Work http://www.waystowork.com/documents/Evaluations/WtW_reference_book.pdf

64 Associated Press. "Devices Can Halt Cars with Tardy Payments." Billings Gazette. 10 April 2005. http://www.billingsgazette.com/newdex.php?display=rednews/2005/10/04/build/business/45-halt-cars.inc

5. Promotion of Fuel-Efficient Vehicles

As more and more people require cars to get to work, fuel-efficient vehicles are becoming essential in mitigating the impact of fuel emissions and air pollution. The types of cars Bonnie CLAC finances—typically Toyota Corollas and Honda Civics—have higher gas mileage, more efficient operating costs, and lower environmental impacts.[65] For example, a 1998 Subaru Legacy consumes 20% more gasoline, produces 20% more in greenhouse emissions, and gets 20% fewer miles per gallon than a 2007 Toyota Corolla.[66] A Bonnie CLAC car reduces carbon emissions by 36 metric tons of CO_2 over the life of the car.

Bonnie CLAC has received many awards and prizes for its unique and entrepreneurial program (See Bonnie CLAC Appendix 1 on page 144). In the past few years, Bonnie CLAC has been the subject of feature articles in the national media, including *Time, Business Week, The Wall Street Journal,* and *The Washington Post.* Last year, it received The Purpose Prize, a contest sponsored by Civic Ventures which received more than 1,200 submissions nationwide.[67] This year, Bonnie CLAC was awarded the prestigious Manhattan Institute Award for Social Entrepreneurship.[68]

In just six years, Bonnie CLAC has established itself as the premiere nonprofit car program in the country. It has improved the lives of the New Hampshire residents it has served[69] (See Bonnie CLAC Appendix 2 on page 146 for Client Testimonials). But there are 42.5 million very low to moderate income households in the United States, and a quarter of them purchase used cars each year, spending $85 billion at "buy-here, pay-here" dealerships.[70] Bonnie CLAC will use its national expansion to reach this vulnerable population and help them save money and obtain better, more reliable cars toward the overall improvement of their lives and the overall improvement of the environment.

---

65 "Enterprising Ideas: Lending a Hand." NOW. Host David Brancaccio. Public Broadcasting System. 22 June 2007. http://www.pbs.org/now/shows/325/index.html
66 http://www.fueleconomy.gov
67 http://www.purposeprize.org/index.cfm
68 http://www.manhattan-institute.org/html/social_entrepreneurship.htm
69 Ward, Sally and Sarah Savage. "Bonnie CLAC Interview Analysis." Carsey Institute, University of New Hampshire, Fall 2007.
70 Automotive News Data Center, CNW Marketing/Research and ADESA Analytical Services. 42.5 million very low to moderate income households divided by four (a quarter of households purchase cars each year) = 10.6 million very low to moderate income households * $7,998 (average price of used car) = $85 billion.

II. SOCIAL INNOVATION IN ACTION: THE BONNIE CLAC OPERATING MODEL

Bonnie CLAC Operating Model

Bonnie CLAC currently operates one district in Lebanon, New Hampshire, with five satellite sites located in Keene, Manchester, Concord, Portsmouth, and Exeter (see Bonnie CLAC Appendix 3 on page 147).

Bonnie CLAC's proven, comprehensive car-purchase program uses a seven-step process to help its very low to moderate income clients obtain reliable cars at affordable prices. The seven steps are: 1) Recruiting, 2) Screening, 3) One-on-One Counseling or FastTrack, 4) Vehicle Selection, 5) Financing, 6) Delivery of a New Car, and 7) Alumni Support (see Figure B below).

Figure B: The Bonnie CLAC Program Model

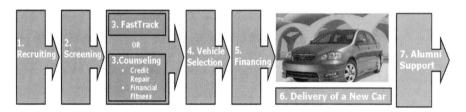

Throughout the process, Bonnie CLAC Client Consultants meet regularly with clients to provide step-by-step guidance. This one-on-one relationship, and the trust that results from this close bond, make Bonnie CLAC unique and effective in working with this often-challenging population. Other personnel involved in the process include an Intake Manager who screens calls, a Financial Fitness Instructor who teaches financial literacy classes, a BRIDGE Manager who provides transitional loaner cars to clients who need them while they complete the program, and a Delivery Manager who supports car selection, completes the necessary financing paperwork and manages the delivery of the new car upon program completion. For a detailed description of each step of the process, see below or in Bonnie CLAC Appendix 4 on page 147.

1. Recruiting

Bonnie CLAC recruits prospects from the very low to moderate income community. Local offices work with social service agencies to find prospective clients, partner with and make local company presentations, and distribute flyers to spread the word about Bonnie CLAC.

2a. Screening I:

After an initial inquiry comes in, Bonnie CLAC's Intake Manager uses a short, telephone-based survey to determine whether the prospect has at least $300 in disposable income after paying monthly expenses. This screening process helps ensure that those who come in for a Client Consultant interview have a good chance of enrolling and succeeding in the Bonnie CLAC program.

2b. Screening II:

Prospects who are approved over the telephone are invited to come to a local site and meet personally with a Client Consultant. They are asked to bring income and expense statements with them so the consultant can verify whether they have sufficient disposable income to meet monthly car, insurance, and gas payments. The goal of this meeting is to ascertain financial qualifications and to help prospects better understand the program so they can decide whether or not to enroll. Prospects who choose to enroll pay a $65 fee and become official Bonnie CLAC clients.

3. FastTrack or Counseling:

As soon as a client enters the program, the enrolling Client Consultant becomes his/her counselor. The Client Consultant works with the client to develop a customized plan that fits the client's personal financial status and situation. Clients with good to excellent credit records, stable employment, and residence history may enter FastTrack and receive a new car almost immediately. Otherwise, clients begin an intensive counseling program that includes credit repair, Financial Fitness (FinFit) classes, and other needed assignments required by the individual's profile.

- Credit Repair

  Client Consultants perform one-on-one credit analysis to determine the credit counseling appropriate for each client. The customized clean-up plan is based on the client's credit history and his/her ability to make payments to creditors. Clients whose accounts are in collection can take 6-12 months to improve their credit history. During this time, Client Consultants will give clients "assignments" toward credit repair and (re)establishment of a positive payment history.

» Credit repair assignments may include paying charged-off loans, making plans to pay all regular monthly expenses (rent, utilities, loans, etc.) on time, explaining medical charge-offs, and identifying fraud or errors and correcting them.

» (Re)establishment of a positive payment history may include the creation of a savings plan and/or enrollment in Bonnie CLAC's transitional BRIDGE car program.

▫ During the savings plan, clients are required to deposit $250-$285 per month into a savings account, with the purpose of demonstrating their ability to build this recurring "expense" into their budget.

▫ The BRIDGE program provides clients who need a "bridge" loaner car with one at a cost of only $250 a month. At the same time, clients improve their credit records by building a history of on-time, monthly payments. The BRIDGE Manager places clients into this program, lines up the necessary BRIDGE cars for them, collects monthly payments, and conducts a review after two to three months. The BRIDGE Manager also helps transition BRIDGE clients into the next step of the program once their credit records have been sufficiently repaired.

- Financial Fitness (FinFit)[71]

Financial Fitness (FinFit) is a five-week financial literacy program taught by a Bonnie CLAC FinFit Instructor. FinFit classes include budgeting and financial goal setting, checking-account management, money-saving techniques, protecting and building a positive credit history, and food economics and nutrition. Food economics and nutrition is included as a topic of Financial Fitness because Bonnie CLAC strives to help clients make economic shopping choices and improve health outcomes. Financial Fitness teaches clients to make sustainable changes in all aspects of their lives by encouraging personal growth related to self-worth and status, long-term planning and thinking, and the development of a healthy relationship to money.

---

71 www.bonnieclac.org and through discussions with Bonnie CLAC's FinFit Instructors. The FinFit classes have a high satisfaction rate among students and have been praised by local educators and officials.

4. Vehicle Selection:

The client and Client Consultant work together to select a vehicle that is appropriate for the client's budget, family size, and other needs. This selection is usually a Toyota Corolla or a Honda Civic, although other vehicles may be purchased with the approval of the Client Consultant. Bonnie CLAC's focus is on financing fuel-efficient cars. This goal helps combat fuel emissions and pollution even as it puts more very low to moderate income drivers on the road. Once a vehicle has been selected, the Client Consultant asks the Delivery Manager to locate the vehicle.

5. Financing a Car:

Upon completing the program and selecting a car, the client is now ready to purchase the car. The Client Consultant collects the following information in order to advocate for the client in his/her loan application.

- Client's length of time with Bonnie CLAC

- Programs completed with Bonnie CLAC (Credit Repair, Savings Plan, BRIDGE Program, Financial Fitness)

- Time at job

- Time at residence

- Current vehicle/transportation source

- Average weekly commute to work

- Explanation of credit issues

Bonnie CLAC enables its clients to obtain wholesale financing rates for their new car loans through partnerships with financial institutions. Bonnie CLAC acts as guarantor for the car loan. Interest rates average around 6.8%, which is exceptionally low for this particular client base.[72] Once the loan is submitted and approved by the financial institution, Bonnie CLAC's Delivery Manager completes the purchase and sale documentation and the bank loan paperwork necessary for the purchase of the new car. Clients sign a lease for a five-year loan, with monthly payments of $250-$285. Each client also pays a one-time loan

---

72 Vogel: 4.

guarantor's fee of $800 to Bonnie CLAC for financing and providing support throughout the duration of the loan. This $800 is built into the terms of the loan instead of coming directly out of the client's pocket.

6. Delivery of a New Car:

When the loan has been funded and the money has been paid to the car dealership, the Delivery Coordinator either accompanies the client to the local dealership to pick up the new car, or arranges for the local car dealership to drop it off.

7. Alumni Support:

Once Bonnie CLAC clients receive their new cars, they are known as Bonnie CLAC alumni. Bonnie CLAC alumni are contacted periodically by Client Consultants for follow-up and monitoring throughout the life of the car loan. This includes information or assistance with:

- Maintenance, repairs, warranties, and/or extended warranties
- Disputes with insurance companies over unfair claim decisions
- Communications with the financial institution regarding car loans
- Ongoing financial fitness support and education
- Discounts on new and used auto parts
- Preparations for future car purchases

Financial Health

Bonnie CLAC's comprehensive and holistic approach has proven it can be a successful operating model. In 2006, 204 new car transactions were completed by Bonnie CLAC. The district earned over $200,000 by charging a $65 enrollment fee, an $800 car transaction fee, and a $200 loan origination fee for each car successfully provided.

However, Bonnie CLAC has reached only a small percentage of its potential market, leaving ample room for growth. The rest of this business plan will focus on Bonnie CLAC's five-year growth strategy.

III. BONNIE CLAC'S GROWTH STRATEGY

Figure C below summarizes Bonnie CLAC's Social Impact Model, which will guide the organization's growth strategy over the next five years. The model states the social problem that Bonnie CLAC addresses, along with the organization's mission in meeting that need. It goes on to describe Bonnie CLAC's operating model and sets forth Bonnie CLAC's five-pronged strategy to grow district by district across the country. Finally, the Social Impact Model outlines the organizational, program performance, and social and economic indicators that Bonnie CLAC will track to measure its success toward achieving the overall vision. The feedback loop shows how Bonnie CLAC will continuously monitor the success of its operating model and social impact strategies so it can make course corrections along the way. (For a more complete view of the Social Impact Model, see Bonnie CLAC Appendix 5 on page 152.)

Figure C: Bonnie CLAC Social Impact Model

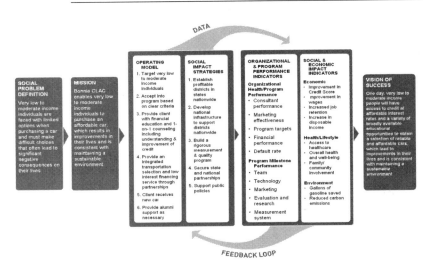

The foundation of the Social Impact Model is Bonnie CLAC's core mission, vision, and the five operational strategies that will guide its activities.

MISSION

Bonnie CLAC enables very low to moderate income individuals to purchase an affordable car, which results in improvements in their lives and is consistent with maintaining a sustainable environment.

VISION

One day, very low to moderate income people will have access to credit at affordable interest rates and a variety of broadly available educational opportunities to obtain a selection of reliable and affordable cars, which lead to improvements in their lives and is consistent with maintaining a sustainable environment.

OPERATIONAL STRATEGIES

- Establish profitable districts that will contribute financially toward national operations
- Develop the infrastructure needed to support national expansion
- Implement a rigorous measurement & quality program
- Develop state and national partnerships
- Support public policies

Choosing a Scale Strategy—The 'Branch' Model

The Bonnie CLAC operating model has been developed and tested over time to ensure success. Replicating this model successfully requires choosing the core elements of the plan while allowing other elements to remain optional. The overall goal, particularly in Phase I, is to protect the integrity and quality of the model while allowing for adjustments to be made according to locality that will increase the chances of success.

Pathways to Social Impact: Strategies for Scaling Out Successful Social Innovations, a paper from Duke University's Center for the Advancement of Social Entrepreneurship, describes two key considerations when developing a replication strategy: 1) what to replicate and 2) how to replicate. Bonnie CLAC's model is complex and comprehensive; therefore, it has chosen a branch model to ensure that the model can be closely monitored and adjusted by the national office during its initial replication phase (see Figure D). In addition, it has chosen a branch model because there are great efficiencies that can be gained from having many functions performed at the national level to provide economies of scale and a greater chance for district success[73] (see Figure D).

---

73 Dees, J.G., Anderson, B. and Wei-Skillern, J. (Aug 2002). *Pathways to Social Impact: Strategies for Scaling Out Successful Social Innovations.* Center for the Advancement of Social Entrepreneurship, The Fuqua School of Business, Duke University.

Figure D: Social Innovation Matrix

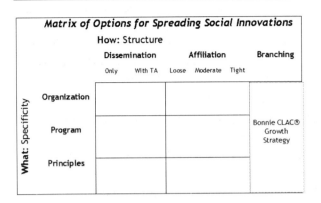

As seen below in Figure E, each new Bonnie CLAC district will become part of Bonnie CLAC national. All the districts will operate along the lines of the current Lebanon, New Hampshire, district, striving toward specific targets of operational efficiency and financial profitability.

The branch model provides Bonnie CLAC with the best path toward building efficient operations and maintaining quality control, while also improving model replication. The national office will continuously monitor the replication of new districts to make course corrections or to disseminate best practices.

Figure E: Bonnie CLAC Organizational Model

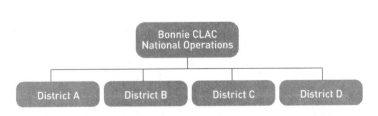

Business Plan Timeline

The business plan is structured into three phases over five plus years. Details in this business plan will focus on Phase I and cover two years, from January 2008 to December 2009. The goals in each phase are listed in Table D.

Table D: Goals by Phase

PHASES	GOALS
PHASE I: Piloting new districts in select New England states and building national support systems Jan 2008–Dec 2009 (2 Years)	▪ Launch four new districts ▪ Solidify national leadership team and operations ▪ Build a robust measurement and quality system ▪ Establish initial state and national partnerships ▪ Begin public policy work
PHASE II: Testing growth of districts nationwide Jan 2010–Dec 2011 (2 Years)	▪ Make necessary course corrections for district model ▪ Select sites and test district model beyond New England
PHASE III: Scaling Nationwide 2012 (1+ Years)	▪ Scale Bonnie CLAC operations nationwide

In Phase I, from January 2008 through December 2009, the current Lebanon, New Hampshire, district will serve as Bonnie CLAC's flagship model district, to support the training and development of all future districts. Current national operations will also be strengthened to support district growth. Four additional districts will be launched during Phase I, with one new district each in Massachusetts and Maine. The remaining two New England locations have yet to be determined based on further information collected in 2008.

In Phase II, from 2010-2012, Bonnie CLAC will launch 21 new districts, completing its expansion across New England and beginning nationwide expansion.

In Phase III, beyond 2012, Bonnie CLAC will scale districts across the United States. It expects to launch districts at a rapid pace based on knowledge gained and improvements made over the previous four years.

By the end of 2012, Bonnie CLAC will have a total of 26 districts in operation. It will have provided 8,117 clients with new cars since its founding, financed nearly $121.8 million in car loans, and saved clients an estimated $16.2 million. In addition, it will have prevented more than 78,800 metric tons of CO_2 from being released into the atmosphere, the equivalent of taking 17,060 passenger cars off the roads for a year or preserving 646 acres of forest from deforestation[74] (see Table E). In addition, Bonnie CLAC brings about many positive, long-term social and economic outcomes, such as improvements to health, family, personal well-being, wages, and credit scores, discussed in greater detail in Section IX of this business plan.

Table E: Annual Outcomes

YEAR	2001–2007	2008	2009	2010	2011	2012	Total
Districts Opened		1	3	5	7	9	25
Total Number of Districts	1	2	5	10	17	26	26
Number of Clients Receiving Cars	1040	280	474	963	1,875	3,485	8,117
Amount of Financing Secured [1]		$4.2mm	$7.1mm	$14.4mm			$121.8 mm
Savings by Clients [2]	$2 mm		$948,000	$1.9mm	$3.8mm	$7.0mm	$16.2mm
Carbon Reduction (metric tons)	30,137	5,080	6,880	10,483	13,608	12,646	78,834

[1] Assumes an average loan of $15,000.
[2] Annual savings calculated in Table C.
[3] Assumes Bonnie CLAC cars average an increase of 8 mpg over client's previous car.

74 U.S. Climate Technology Corporation Gateway (http://www.usctcgateway.net/tool/)

BUSINESS PLAN IMPLEMENTATION: OPERATIONAL GROWTH STRATEGIES

Phase I Goal: Piloting New Districts in Select New England States & Building National Support Systems, 2 Years (January 2008–December 2009)

A. Launch Four New Districts

Phase I Goal: Establish New Hampshire as the flagship district site and pilot four additional districts, all working towards profitability and contributing to the national office operational budget.

1. Establish New Hampshire as the Flagship District

New Hampshire will serve as the flagship district for Bonnie CLAC operations. Some of the responsibilities of the flagship district include:

- Documenting and fine-tuning the model for district operation

- Developing training and operational manuals for other districts (see Bonnie CLAC Appendix 6 on page 153)

- Providing training to other district sites

- Testing district innovations:

  » Utilizing volunteers as client consultants

  » Opening a satellite office in remote areas

  » Outsourcing FinFit classes

- Serving as the host model site for organizations or parties interested in launching a district office

2. Pilot Four New Districts

Using New Hampshire as a model, Bonnie CLAC has carefully studied the best way to select a district site and grow it toward profitability. Bonnie CLAC has created a district financial growth model that will allow each new district to become profitable in Year 4. This model uses the following key assumptions, which were determined using Bonnie CLAC's historical records:

a. Piloting a District

- A Bonnie CLAC district will have the following growth in completed car transactions: Year 1) 25, Year 2) 80, Year 3) 200, Year 4) 300, Year 5) 400

- 75% of clients will come from very low to moderate income households; 25% of clients will come from above moderate income households

- Clients will take an average of six months to go through the program

- At full capacity, a Client Consultant can serve 140 clients per year

- In order to ensure that a district can both fund district expenses and eventually provide financial support for national operations, Bonnie CLAC is setting clear targets for its marketing efforts. Those assumptions are as follows:

  » 75% very low to moderate income clients:

    ▫ 25% of households in a district are looking for a car

    ▫ 6% of that market will inquire about Bonnie CLAC each year

    ▫ 65% will pass the initial phone screen

    ▫ 35% of those who have a one-on-one interview will enroll in the program

    ▫ 85% will complete the program and receive a new car

  » 25% above moderate income households:

    ▫ 25% of households in a district are looking for a car

    ▫ 6% of that market will inquire about Bonnie CLAC each year

    ▫ 100% will pass the initial phone screen

    ▫ 100% who have a one-on-one interview will enroll in the program

    ▫ 100% will complete the program and receive a new car

Based on these assumptions, a district requires a market of approximately 60,000 very low to moderate income households and approximately 200 car transactions to become profitable in Year 3. By Year 5, a district that covers 120,000 very low to moderate income households and completes 400 car transactions will contribute over $80,000 to national operations (see Table F).

The social return on investment is quite impressive. For a $170,000 one-time investment in a new Bonnie CLAC district, approximately

1,000 clients will receive new cars and save a cumulative $2,000,000 over five years (Table F). This figure does not even take into account the many positive social and economic improvements to health, family, personal well-being, wages, and credit scores that accrue to Bonnie CLAC alumni in the long term. (See Section IX for further discussion of long-term outcomes).

Table F: Bonnie CLAC Start-up District Office Operations

	Phase I		Phase II		
	2008	2009	2010	2011	2012
Revenues	28,840	93,136	225,900	337,028	447,710
Expenses	118,202	144,947	223,591	298,941	365,374
Net Income	(89,362)	(51,811)	2,309	38,087	82,336
Total Households	8,000	24,000	60,000	90,000	120,000
Car Transactions	25	80	200	300	400
Client Savings	$50,000	$160,000	$400,000	$600,000	$800,000

3. Selecting and Locating Districts (Bonnie CLAC Appendix 7)

In Phase I, Bonnie CLAC will launch four new districts in the New England region. To select the most promising states in which to locate its prospective districts, Bonnie CLAC will use the following process:

a. Determine which states within each region have the highest number of very low to moderate income households (see Table H).

b. Determine which states have the greatest fundraising capability.

c. Determine which states have the greatest partnership support and potential.

Using the process above, Bonnie CLAC has determined that its first two new districts will be located in Massachusetts and Maine.

In locating the district office within a qualifying state, Bonnie CLAC will use the following process:

a. Use HUD guidelines and the US Census to determine the cities that have very low to moderate income populations of 120,000 households or more.[75] Examples of cities in Massachusetts and Maine that fit this criteria are shown in Table G below:

Table G: Very Low to Moderate Income Households in MA & ME

Metropolitan Statistical Area [1]	Median Household Income	Very Low Upper Limit (30%)	Low Upper Limit (50%)	Moderate Upper Limit (80%)	Radius	# Very Low to Moderate Income Households [2]
MASSACHUSETTS						
Worcester, MA/CT	$ 55,595	$ 16,679	$ 27,798	$ 44,476	50	1,255,970
Boston/Cambridge/Quincy, MA/NH	$ 62,678	$ 18,803	$ 31,339	$ 50,142	50	1,186,650
Providence/Fall River/Warwick MA/RI	$ 51,664	$ 15,499	$ 25,832	$ 41,331	50	1,077,098
Manchester, NH/MA	$ 59,102	$ 17,731	$ 29,551	$ 47,282	50	728,553
New Bedford, MA	$ 44,252	$ 13,276	$ 22,126	$ 35,402	50	694,883
Springfield, MA/CT	$ 45,902	$ 13,771	$ 22,951	$ 36,722	50	638,872
Pittsfield, MA	$ 52,113	$ 15,634	$ 26,057	$ 41,690	50	422,029
Barnstable Town, MA	$ 54,328	$ 16,298	$ 27,164	$ 43,462	50	259,354
MAINE						
Portsmouth, NH/ME	$ 59,680	$ 17,904	$ 29,840	$ 47,744	50	533,430
Portland/S. Portland/Biddeford ME	$ 48,883	$ 14,665	$ 24,442	$ 39,106	50	190,563
Lewiston/Auburn, ME	$ 43,455	$ 13,037	$ 21,728	$ 34,764	50	181,018
FLAGSHIP DISTRICT						
Lebanon, NH/VT [3]	$ 41,953	$ 12,586	$ 20,977	$ 33,562	50	128,582

[1] Income by metropolitan statistical area from American Community Survey 2005 of the US Census
http://factfinder.census.gov/servlet/ADPGeoSearchByListServlet?ds_name=ACS_2005_EST_G00_&_lang=en&_ts=200697026088
[2] Number of very low to moderate income households for a 50-mile radius calculated using US Decennial Census.
[3] Lebanon, NH/VT data calculated using US Decennial Census.

b. Determine which districts have the greatest fundraising capability. At a minimum, a district office must be able to raise $100,000 in start-up philanthropic funds to launch and an additional $70,000 in the next 18 months.

c. Determine which districts have the greatest partnership support and potential. Each district office must be supported by:

   i. 2-3 social service and nonprofit referral agencies

   ii. 2-3 corporations that hire or serve a population fitting Bonnie CLAC's target profile

   iii. At least one organization that can teach high-quality financial fitness classes

   iv. At least one organization willing to provide in-kind office facilities for a start-up staff for the next two years

   v. 1 financing bank (if necessary)

---

75 Note: Census information at the city level (called metropolitan statistical areas) can be found using http://factfinder.census.gov/servlet/ADPGeoSearchByListServlet?ds_name=ACS_2005_EST_G00_&_lang=en&_ts=200697026088

d. Other criteria, such as distance to and from public transportation, centrality of location, or political considerations, may be taken into account at the discretion of the Regional Director and CEO.

Bonnie CLAC will locate the first new districts in areas close to its current flagship district office in Lebanon, NH. It will use these new district offices to develop best practices and strengthen its ability to launch additional districts in Phase II.

4. Expanding within a District

The district office in each state will serve as the central hub, and satellite office sites will emanate as spokes from a hub (see Figure F below). Satellite office sites may not have brick and mortar office facilities; instead, Client Consultants will operate mobilely, using a laptop, a cellular phone, and an automobile.

Figure F: District & Satellite/Hub & Spoke Expansion Model

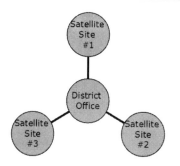

It is important to understand that there are expenses involved in launching each new satellite location. Therefore, satellite locations will be launched according to the following capacity guidelines:

1. Bonnie CLAC will add client consultants in a district only when existing client consultant(s) in that district are operating at 80% of capacity.

2. Bonnie CLAC will open additional satellite sites within a district only when existing sites in that district have achieved 3% penetration of the relevant market area.

3. Bonnie CLAC will use the same criteria of market size and partnership potential in identifying potential satellite sites.

4. Bonnie CLAC will select those sites in closest proximity to existing district and satellite offices as the next location for a satellite office.

5. When the district area has been saturated (i.e. approaching 400 car transactions per year), a satellite site may be re-aligned into a new district that will now create its own new satellite offices.

B. Solidify National Leadership Team and Operations

Phase I Goal: Build a national leadership team that will put systems, policies, and procedures in place, refine the marketing strategy, build an alumni network, and utilize technology in order to build the highly-efficient operations required to scale nationally

Action areas in this phase will consist of the following five key areas of activity:

1. Build a National Leadership Team

In Phase I, Bonnie CLAC will build a Senior Management Team, consisting of a President, Chief Executive Officer, Chief Marketing Officer, Director of Measurement and Quality, and Director of Training and Human Resources. Further descriptions of each position can be found in the Team section (Section IV) of the business plan.

2. Put Systems, Policies, and Procedures in Place

In Phase I, Bonnie CLAC will put systems, policies, and procedures in place so the organization is better positioned to scale. Areas to be analyzed and strengthened include: financial reporting; fundraising; legal matters, including trademarks and contracts; and systems and communications between national and district offices and between district and satellite offices.

Bonnie CLAC will test out three partnership options for scaling its BRIDGE car program:

1. Bonnie CLAC will buy 10 good used cars (5 for the flagship Lebanon, New Hampshire, district and 5 for the first new district to be launched in Year 1) at $6,000 each, using a grant from the New Hampshire Community Development Finance Authority (CDFA). Monthly BRIDGE payments will be placed into a fund for the purchase of replacement BRIDGE cars on a periodic basis.

2. Bonnie CLAC will develop and test a subleasing partnership with a national car rental company (i.e. Enterprise, Avis, Budget, Alamo, National, Dollar, Thrifty, or Hertz) or a national used car rental company offering discount prices, such as Rent-A-Wreck.

3. Bonnie CLAC will develop and test a car purchase program with car manufacturer Honda or Toyota. Bonnie CLAC will finance the new cars in monthly installments, to be paid by the clients' monthly BRIDGE payment fees.

At the conclusion of the test in Year 1, Bonnie CLAC will select the most cost effective and scalable BRIDGE option to implement across all of its district offices. The option selected should not have a significant detrimental effect on Bonnie CLAC's finances.

In addition, emphasis will be placed on human resources, including the creation of hiring, training, development, and evaluation policies and procedures at the national and district levels. Information about these areas can be found throughout the rest of the business plan.

3. Refine the Marketing Strategy

Bonnie CLAC will craft a clear brand and communications strategy and develop a target consumer profile to identify Bonnie CLAC's most promising clients. In Phase I, Bonnie CLAC will test three strategies to more effectively reach these target clients, consisting of referrals, district partnerships, and direct marketing. More details can be found in the Marketing section (Section VI) of the business plan.

4. Build an Alumni Network

Bonnie CLAC follows up with its clients after the car purchase transaction and supports its clients through the five-year life of the loan. The Chief Marketing Officer will work with Regional Directors to build an alumni network and maintain a regular schedule of alumni contact, including alumni outreach newsletters, organized alumni events, and other alumni activities.

5. Strengthen Technology Systems

In Phase I, Bonnie CLAC will strengthen its technology systems so they are better able to support all aspects of the organization as it grows. Bonnie CLAC will engage a third-party to review its long-term information technology needs. This review will be designed to identify current deficiencies in Bonnie CLAC's technology systems and make the necessary improvements for scaling.

As part of its technology review, Bonnie CLAC will assess the functionality of Bonnie CLAC Cars™ (its current QuickBase database system) as a scalable application capable of handling both district and national operations. It will identify performance gaps in the system, develop a plan to address these gaps, and acquire the necessary technology to meet the organization's future needs.

More details about technology can be found in Section V of the business plan.

C. Build a Robust Measurement and Quality System

Phase I Goal: Develop the necessary dashboard(s) and processes to establish a coordinated program of organizational-health, program-performance, and social and economic impact measurement.

Action areas in this phase will focus on three core activities:

1. Measurement and Quality System

In Phase I, Bonnie CLAC will develop a self-evaluation system that measures ongoing performance of both district and national operations as well as the long-term impact it has on the lives of its clients and the environment. The implementation of this system will include a feedback loop that allows Bonnie CLAC to evaluate its performance at regular intervals and make necessary adjustments to improve performance.

2. Third-Party Evaluations

Bonnie CLAC is currently undergoing its first third-party evaluation. Conducted by the Carsey Institute at the University of New Hampshire, this outside evaluation will culminate in a published report in Winter 2007. (The preliminary interview guide, preliminary interview results, and the final survey instrument are located in Bonnie CLAC Appendices 8, 9 and 10). In Phase I, Bonnie CLAC will build upon the initial third-party evaluation. Bonnie CLAC will hire a long-term third-party evaluator to track the longitudinal impact of its work. These efforts will validate the credibility of Bonnie CLAC's program and enable the organization to attract government and other support in future years.

3. Research Agenda

In Phase I, Bonnie CLAC will explore the possibility of working with academic institutions and/or professors to develop a research agenda. The agenda would identify research questions to be answered, such as the long-term effects of reliable transportation or the availability of car financing for very low to moderate income individuals. Bonnie CLAC would offer its academic partners access to its proprietary dataset so researchers could produce white papers that answer these questions and contribute to policy awareness of very low to moderate income needs.

D. Establish Initial State & National Partnerships

Phase I Goal: Develop state and national partnerships that prepare Bonnie CLAC to scale.

Bonnie CLAC will develop mutually beneficial state and national partnerships with the following categories of organizations in order to increase efficiencies of the operating model and to develop additional funding sources in preparation to scale.

- Car manufacturers

- Financial institutions

- Media outlets

- Nonprofit organizations

- Government agencies

Partnership strategy will be discussed in greater detail in Sections VI and VII of the business plan.

E. Support Public Policy

Phase I Goal: Develop focused initiatives to support state and federal public policies that further the organization's mission and vision.

Bonnie CLAC plans to focus on the following public policy areas:

- Transportation Individual Development Accounts (TIDAs)

- The ability for TANF (Temporary Assistance for Needy Families) recipients to own cars worth more than $4,000

- A federal one-time earned income tax credit (EITC) to be used for the purchase of a reliable, affordable car through a nonprofit organization

In addition, Bonnie CLAC will form alliances with state and federal government agencies, national foundations, and other nonprofit organizations to focus on additional initiatives that will impact the organization's mission and vision. These agency and foundation alliances are discussed in greater detail in the public policy section (Section X) of the business plan.

Phase II: Testing Growth of Districts Nationwide, 2 Years (January 2010–December 2011)

In Phase II, 2010 through 2011, Bonnie CLAC will launch an additional 21 districts throughout the remaining New England states and other states nationwide. Table H shows the total number of very low to moderate income households in each state. This table confirms the vast market opportunity of approximately 42.5 million very low to moderate income households (or 40.0 million households excluding New England) that form the target market for Bonnie CLAC's services.

Table H: Number of Very Low to Moderate Income Households by US State

State	Very Low Income Upper Limit [1]	Low Income Upper Limit [1]	Moderate Income Upper Limit [1]	# of Households (Less than $10,000)	# of Households ($10,000 to $14,999)	# of Households ($15,000 to $24,999)	# of Households ($25,000 to $34,999)	# of Households ($35,000 to $49,999)	Total # of Very Low to Moderate Income Households [2]	Sufficient Market Size?
Alabama	$11,450	$19,100	$30,550	219,792	146,731	263,520	222,085		852,128	Y
Alaska	$17,050	$28,450	$45,500	14,570	10,256	22,553	20,969	32,625	101,073	N
Arizona	$11,450	$19,050	$30,500	168,348	130,348	283,041	279,190		860,927	Y
Arkansas	$10,400	$17,350	$27,750	130,025	93,518	168,254			391,797	Y
California	$14,075	$23,490	$37,525	833,171	636,652	1,294,132	1,204,271		3,968,226	Y
Colorado	$13,850	$23,050	$36,900	129,656	95,104	201,502	197,491		623,753	Y
Connecticut	$19,450	$32,400	$50,050	87,610	64,372	108,185	118,208	165,675	544,050	Y
Delaware	$14,000	$23,300	$37,300	18,415	15,508	32,848	33,069		99,841	N
Florida	$13,050	$21,750	$34,800	586,067	453,396	925,403	921,025		2,885,891	Y
Georgia	$12,200	$20,350	$32,550	314,355	197,173	385,463	384,453		1,281,444	Y
Hawaii	$15,050	$30,050	$48,100	27,519	19,915	33,378	41,080	63,355	185,347	Y
Idaho	$12,250	$20,450	$32,700	43,620	35,652	74,626	70,752		224,650	Y
Illinois	$13,650	$22,750	$36,400	371,174	266,276	507,756	508,454		1,653,662	Y
Indiana	$14,675	$24,475	$39,150	198,490	155,500	303,232	311,933		968,365	Y
Iowa	$13,400	$22,350	$35,750	87,839	76,405	161,124	149,412		474,780	Y
Kansas	$12,700	$21,150	$33,850	86,767	68,013	141,445	136,569		432,794	Y
Kentucky	$11,150	$18,550	$29,700	203,184	138,293	229,331			570,808	Y
Louisiana	$11,200	$18,650	$29,850	221,340	144,887	238,360			605,087	Y
Maine	$13,175	$21,975	$35,150	48,390	39,256	67,253	69,491		224,390	Y
Maryland	$17,600	$29,700	$47,500	121,378	90,851	164,925	184,086	284,333	845,573	Y
Mass.	$20,150	$33,600	$50,050	200,348	132,143	225,458	209,692	301,864	1,069,505	Y
Michigan	$13,250	$22,050	$35,300	333,374	237,146	468,242	456,276		1,495,038	Y
Minnesota	$13,850	$23,100	$36,950	126,831	103,988	207,177	215,873		653,919	Y
Mississippi	$10,150	$16,900	$27,050	162,505	92,582	163,514			418,501	Y
Missouri	$11,100	$18,500	$29,600	207,845	150,953	305,118			663,916	Y
Montana	$11,750	$19,550	$31,300	34,015	28,938	53,434	49,580		165,967	Y
Nebraska	$12,650	$21,050	$33,700	55,912	43,157	87,883	92,168		279,130	Y
Nevada	$15,150	$25,250	$40,400	62,202	46,654	100,733	106,106		315,695	Y
New Hampshire	$17,700	$29,500	$47,200	28,747	22,168	42,044	49,444	72,156	214,559	Y
N. Jersey	$20,500	$34,200	$50,050	198,079	147,438	275,368	262,183	396,467	1,279,555	Y
N. Mexico	$10,200	$17,000	$27,200	82,072	54,676	107,347			244,095	Y
N. York	$14,775	$24,625	$39,400	699,245	424,179	779,196	719,593		2,622,213	Y
N. Carolina	$12,475	$20,800	$33,275	340,741	239,249	462,682	437,167		1,479,839	Y
N. Dakota	$11,900	$19,850	$31,750	24,740	17,888	36,632	34,945		114,205	N
Ohio	$14,200	$23,650	$37,850	408,366	293,117	572,108	547,599		1,821,790	Y
Oklahoma	$10,900	$18,150	$29,050	155,262	108,511	203,292			467,065	Y
Oregon	$12,375	$20,625	$33,000	126,553	97,247	181,992	174,035		579,827	Y
Pennsylvania	$13,150	$19,025	$35,100	415,384	323,681	623,945	569,530		1,932,540	Y
Rhode Island	$17,950	$29,900	$47,850	33,638	28,576	39,862	40,875	55,004	197,954	Y
S. Carolina	$12,375	$20,600	$32,975	180,923	118,153	230,542	209,855		739,473	Y
S. Dakota	$12,000	$20,000	$32,000	28,282	21,679	44,587	41,010		135,558	Y
Tenn	$11,700	$19,500	$31,200	265,621	176,795	325,323	309,554		1,077,793	Y
Texas	$11,425	$19,025	$30,450	771,318	554,036	1,043,443	970,161		3,338,958	Y
Utah	$13,200	$22,000	$35,200	48,030	36,570	87,949	99,664		272,213	Y
Vermont	$17,300	$28,800	$46,100	19,516	16,543	28,133	30,736	39,157	134,245	Y
Virginia	$14,150	$23,550	$37,700	210,333	137,114	278,346	291,306		917,099	Y
Washington	$13,650	$22,750	$36,400	183,360	134,657	274,954	269,395		862,566	Y
W. Virginia	$10,600	$17,650	$28,250	95,438	66,105	121,391			282,984	Y
Wisconsin	$14,250	$23,750	$38,000	152,775	130,800	258,545	267,487		809,907	Y
Wyoming	$13,650	$22,750	$36,400	13,255	12,230	25,674	23,878		75,037	N
TOTAL				9,577,231	6,875,878	13,262,527	11,336,758	1,418,646	42,456,232	Y

[1] All upper limits for each state represent the median of income limits for very low, low, and moderate income for all counties in that state. Information from http://www.hud.gov/offices/policy/sections/income/form/2005dcgaslincomelimits.xls
[2] # of households in each income bracket from US Census Bureau "2005 American Community Survey." http://factfinder.census.gov/servlet/DatasetMainPageServlet?_program=ACS&_submenuId=&_lang=en&_ts=

BUSINESS PLAN IMPLEMENTATION: ORGANIZATIONAL
CAPACITY BUILDING

IV. TEAM & GOVERNANCE

Phase I Goal: Establish national and district office organizational structures and build a national leadership team.

A. Bonnie CLAC National Organizational Structure

In order to prepare Bonnie CLAC for national growth, a Chief Executive Officer will be hired in January 2008. Robert Chambers, the

President, will continue to focus on marketing, fundraising, business development, and public speaking while the CEO will focus on building stable and efficient operations. As the organizational structure of the national office for Phase I, shown below in Figure G, illustrates, Responsibility and resources are heavily concentrated in the national office (see Figure G) while district offices operate on a basic structure. This structure allows Bonnie CLAC to offer centralized support to districts and streamline operations in preparation for growth. Below are an organizational chart and a table showing each national officer's responsibilities.

Figure G: Bonnie CLAC National Organization Chart

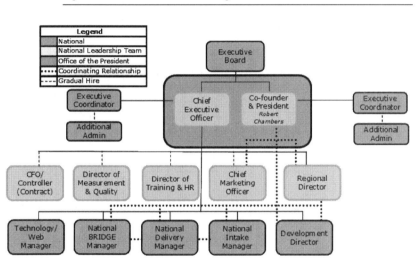

NATIONAL ROLES AND RESPONSIBILITIES (PHASE I)

Executive Board
- Approves and monitors business plan
- Performance review of President and CEO
- Monitors finances
- Supports President and CEO in other areas on an as-requested basis

NATIONAL ROLES AND RESPONSIBILITIES (PHASE I)

Co-Founder and President—Robert Chambers national leadership team	<ul><li>Co-leads the implementation of the business plan, reporting to the Board of Directors (The President and the CEO work closely together and sit in the Office of the President.)</li><li>Leads the development of all national partnerships</li><li>Leads all fundraising activities</li><li>Primary spokesperson for Bonnie CLAC to the public, attending industry, public policy, corporate, nonprofit and fundraising meetings</li><li>Supports the development of marketing</li><li>Supports the development of districts</li></ul>
Chief Executive Officer (hired Jan. 2008) national leadership team	<ul><li>Co-leads the implementation of the business plan, reporting to the Board of Directors (The President and the CEO work very closely together and sit in the Office of the President.)</li><li>Leads the development of all systems for national and district</li><li>Leads the development of all performance measurement systems</li><li>Monitors, reviews, and acts on organizational and program performance indicators at appropriate intervals to ensure that national office and districts are operating efficiently and effectively</li><li>Oversees all national leadership team members except President</li><li>Oversees district operations and manages the Regional Directors</li><li>Ensures a smooth communications and coordinating relationship between national and district offices</li></ul>
Executive Coordinator (hired Jan. 2008)	<ul><li>Assists President, CEO, other Senior Management in carrying out daily functions</li><li>Oversees additional hiring and training of administrative staff as necessary</li></ul>
Executive Assistant (2 Assistants hired Jan. 2009)	<ul><li>Assists Senior Management in carrying out daily functions</li><li>Reports to the Executive Coordinator</li></ul>

NATIONAL ROLES AND RESPONSIBILITIES (PHASE I)

Chief Marketing Officer (hired June 2008) national leadership team	• Leads the development of all marketing activities, with particular emphasis on developing scaling strategies to reach target Bonnie CLAC clients in all districts • Works with CEO and Regional Directors to support district marketing efforts • Works with President to develop and implement national marketing programs
Director of Training and Human Resources (hired Jan. 2008) national leadership team	• Leads the development and implementation of all training for starting and growing districts • Develops, implements, and administers benefit programs for Bonnie CLAC staff • Develops, implements, and administers training and staff development programs • Reviews relevant dashboard indicators with CEO monthly
Director of Measurement & Quality (hired Jun. 2008) national leadership team	• Develops, tracks, analyzes, and publishes organizational-health and program-performance indicators monthly to maintain quality • Collects survey/interview data at appointed intervals to track social and economic indicators • Publishes social and economic indicators on semi-annual basis • Leads the annual process to review indicators and the Social Impact Model to ensure the organization is achieving its mission and vision • Prepares, publishes, and disseminates an annual report card of outcomes • Serves as liaison for all third-party evaluations • Leads the development of a research agenda, which includes fostering relationships with academics and public policy research efforts • Reviews relevant dashboard indicators with CEO monthly

NATIONAL ROLES AND RESPONSIBILITIES (PHASE I)

Technology/Web Manager (hired Apr. 2008)	<ul><li>Updates organization's website, as necessary</li><li>Updates proprietary data management system, Bonnie CLAC Cars™, as necessary in order to continually streamline and improve operational and measurement efficiency as the organization grows</li><li>Updates QuickBooks as necessary in order to incorporate additional functions for financial recordkeeping</li><li>Serves as resource to Senior Management to help them carry out various programs</li><li>Keeps abreast of new technology programs and develops recommended courses of action for purchase and implementation</li><li>Locates and evaluates third-party technology firms/consultants to perform and implement technology reviews as necessary</li><li>Develops standards for computing hardware and software for the organization</li><li>Serves as the point person on all technology issues for the organization</li><li>Reviews relevant dashboard indicators with CEO monthly</li></ul>
Development Director (hired Jan. 2008)	<ul><li>Writes grant proposals</li><li>Supports cultivation and management of philanthropic relationships</li><li>Leads annual fundraising campaign</li><li>Supports all local fundraising efforts</li><li>Develops all marketing materials in conjunction with the Chief Marketing Officer, including collateral, pitch letters, etc.</li><li>Reviews relevant dashboard indicators with CEO monthly</li></ul>
National Intake Manager (hired Jun. 2008)	<ul><li>Conducts all intake interviews to determine eligibility of Bonnie CLAC prospects</li><li>Assigns accepted prospects to one-on-one interviews with local Client Consultants</li><li>Reviews relevant dashboard indicators with CEO monthly</li></ul>

NATIONAL ROLES AND RESPONSIBILITIES (PHASE I)

National BRIDGE Manager (hired Jun. 2008)	• Leads effort to scale the BRIDGE program, by developing relationships with car rental companies and car manufacturers to develop a test program, analyzing test results, and making a recommendation for implementation • Manages BRIDGE program, including responsibility for its bottom line • Coordinates with district offices on BRIDGE car placements, payments, and all other necessary functions • Processes payments, keeps accurate enrollment records, and tracks metrics, including utilization, capacity, and average client tenure, alerting other national staff members if there is a problem • Reviews relevant dashboard indicators with CEO monthly
National Delivery Manager (hired Jun. 2008)	• Completes necessary paperwork for all new car titles • Coordinates with district offices to ensure a smooth and efficient delivery process • Develops extensive knowledge of local auto dealerships • Reviews relevant dashboard indicators with CEO monthly

NATIONAL ROLES AND RESPONSIBILITIES (PHASE II)

Chief Financial Officer / Controller (outsourced part time in Phase I—hired full time in Jan. 2010)	• Prepares accounting and other financial statements for both the national office and district office roll-up • Manages relationships with national lending organizations used by Bonnie CLAC • Helps ensure national office solvency and overall financial health through sound financial record-keeping, analysis, and decision-making • Monitors cash flow and establishes processes to approves expense • Reviews relevant dashboard indicators with CEO monthly

B. Bonnie CLAC District Organizational Structure

In Phase I, a Regional Director will be hired to oversee the New Hampshire flagship district and launch one additional district in 2008. When a new district is launched, it will be staffed by a Lead Client Consultant, who will grow into the role of District Director under the guidance of the Regional Director. At inception, the Client Consultant's role will consist of 50% marketing and 50% direct client work. As the number of clients in the program increases each year and additional Client Consultants are hired, the Lead Client Consultant's role will shift to 80% marketing and 20% direct client work. The Lead Client Consultant will work closely with the National Intake Manager, the National Delivery Manager, and the National BRIDGE Manager to coordinate the intake, delivery, and BRIDGE functions, respectively.

In Phase II, Bonnie CLAC will hire additional Regional Directors to oversee expansion locations. The Regional Directors will work closely with the Director of Training and HR to develop Lead Client Consultants; with the Chief Executive Officer to determine when and where to open new district and satellite offices and to review monthly district dashboard targets; with the Chief Marketing Officer to develop and implement marketing strategies to ensure sufficient client outreach to achieve set targets; and with the Development Director to coordinate local fundraising. Below are a district organizational chart and each staff member's responsibilities within a district.

Figure H: Bonnie CLAC Phase I District Organization Chart

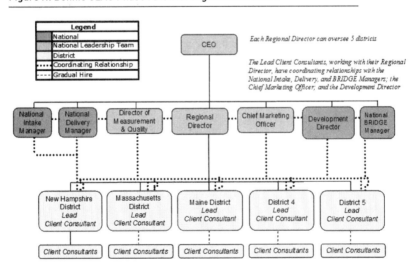

DISTRICT GROWTH ROLES AND RESPONSIBILITIES

Regional Director (to be hired Jan. 2008)	<ul><li>Oversees regional operations and launches and grows new district offices</li><li>Works with the Director of Training and HR to develop lead client consultants into District Directors</li><li>Reviews district dashboards monthly with the Chief Executive Officer, the District's District Directors, and possibly the District's Client Consultants</li><li>Working with the CMO, distributes marketing collateral, press releases, and other promotional materials designed to help fill the regional pipeline</li><li>Establishes necessary regional partnerships</li><li>Works with Development Director on local fundraising efforts</li></ul>
Lead Client Consultant (hired at start of each new district)	<ul><li>Responsible for the success of the district, from its day-to-day operations to its strategic objectives and financial health</li><li>Hires, manages, and develops district staff</li><li>Reviews district dashboards monthly with the Regional Director</li><li>Working with the Regional Director, distributes marketing collateral, press releases, and other promotional materials designed to help fill the pipeline</li><li>Establishes necessary district partnerships</li><li>Each district office will launch with a lead client consultant, who may grow into the role of District Director.</li><li>At inception, the role will consist of 50% marketing and 50% client consulting work, to become 80/20 when additional client consultants are hired.</li><li>Participates in local fundraising efforts</li></ul>

DISTRICT GROWTH ROLES AND RESPONSIBILITIES

Client Consultant

- Works with District Director to ensure solid target marketing in satellite territory
- Receives client assignments from the National Intake Manager and meets one-on-one with all approved, assigned prospects to enroll them in the program
- Coordinates with National BRIDGE Manager to place clients in BRIDGE cars
- Regularly monitors the progress of each assigned client
- Counsels clients one-on-one to help them attain car ownership
- Monitors loans and performs workouts, as necessary
- Coordinates with National Delivery Manager for car delivery and accompanies the client to the car dealership for car pickup
- Follows up with client to provide support throughout the duration of the loan
- Contacts past clients periodically to promote client referrals
- Maintains a regular schedule of contact with alumni by sending alumni outreach newsletters, organizing alumni events, and planning other alumni activities
- Reviews relevant indicators with Regional Director and/or District Director on a monthly basis

C. Governance

Since its inception in 2001, Bonnie CLAC has benefited from a strong governing board. The Board of Directors still includes both co-founders, who continue to take an active interest in the organization's operations. The role of the Board of Directors is to supervise and advise the management of Bonnie CLAC, doing everything in its power to ensure that the organization carries out its mission in the most efficient and productive manner possible toward the accomplishment of its vision. The Board of Directors meets monthly. In recent years, the Board has diversified its areas of expertise by adding new directors from the fields of financial management and marketing. A Bonnie CLAC alumnus has also joined the Board in the role of client representative in order to provide a client voice and perspective.

The most recent addition to the board is Allan Ferguson, a former venture capitalist. His experience in growing companies will provide insight and experience in overseeing Bonnie CLAC as it scales.

rootCAUSE ⊚

The Board of Directors currently consists of the following (See Bonnie CLAC Appendix 11 on page 167 for short bios):

1. Robert L. Chambers, Hanover, NH. President & Co-Founder of Bonnie CLAC.

2. Mary Burnett, Hinsdale, NH. Executive Director of Bonnie CLAC.

3. Robert E. Field, Sr., Hanover, NH.

4. Leo A. Hamill, Jr. Hanover, NH. Co-Founder of Bonnie CLAC.

5. Robert Hansen, Hanover, NH.

6. David Reeves, Norwich, VT.

7. Judith Richard, Concord, NH.

8. Chandra L. Ribiero, West Lebanon, NH. Bonnie CLAC Client Representative.

9. Rick Sayles, Hanover, NH.

10. Allan Ferguson, Meriden, NH.

Bonnie CLAC is committed to further strengthening its governing board by carrying out the following six actions in Phase I:

1. Develop a consistent process to monitor the execution of the business plan in close coordination with the President and CEO. If the President and the CEO disagree on a specific area of execution of the plan, the issue will be brought to the Board for a final decision.

2. Develop a consistent process to evaluate the President and the CEO of Bonnie CLAC on an annual basis.

3. Add 1-2 new board members in areas such as national fundraising and public policy.

4. Launch a CEO search task force, to be led by Co-founder and Board Director Leo Hamill. (See Bonnie CLAC Appendix 12 on page 169 for the CEO job description).

5. Develop an expanded Bonnie CLAC Advisory Board to represent and promote Bonnie CLAC. Such an expansion could

include adding high-profile members from politics, foundations/ nonprofits, and corporations, who will publicly support Bonnie CLAC and help build relationships in their respective field.

6. Form a formal Audit Committee to review financial matters for Bonnie CLAC on a regular basis.

V. TECHNOLOGY

Phase I Goal: Build upon the organization's current technological infrastructure to be able to scale for growth.

A. Current State

Bonnie CLAC has already established a firm technology foundation upon which to build future growth. Recognizing early on that information technology would become increasingly important for its expansion plans, the organization has worked diligently to build a simple, yet robust, technology infrastructure.

Nearly all recordkeeping at Bonnie CLAC is done electronically. Bonnie CLAC uses a database application to support its operations and a well-known software application for its bookkeeping and financial management.

1. Bonnie CLAC Cars ™

Bonnie CLAC uses a proprietary data management system known as Bonnie CLAC Cars™ which was built with Intuit's QuickBase, a web-based environment used by over 45 of the Fortune 100 companies.[76] QuickBase provides a set of online workgroup applications designed for common business needs that have been customized to support Bonnie CLAC's unique data management requirements.

Bonnie CLAC Cars™ performs the following functions:

- Inbound client call management

- Initial telephone profile intake and client registration

- Financial fitness course registration

- Counseling session logging

---

76 http://www.quickbase.com/p/features/overview.asp

- Appointment and class scheduling

- BRIDGE car recordkeeping

- Donation acceptance

- Correspondence creation and tracking

- Car dealer relations

- Loan processing, including preparation and storage of loan documentation

- Title transfers

- Summarizing and reviewing operational activities

Bonnie CLAC Cars™ is run on high-reliability host computers operated by Intuit. Thus, Bonnie CLAC does not need to install software or maintain data on its local computers or servers for this application. All staff members have access to a desktop computer in a Bonnie CLAC office, or, if they work remotely, a laptop (typically an older model IBM ThinkPad). Using these computers, Client Consultants and other staff members can access Bonnie CLAC Cars™ at anytime using a high-speed Internet connection; and with laptops, anywhere.

Since Bonnie CLAC Cars™ is a hosted QuickBase application, its data is automatically backed up by Intuit. In addition, Bonnie CLAC Cars™ can be modified relatively easily. Bonnie CLAC has been able to meet its changing needs by adding new data types and content as necessary.

With a flexible technology infrastructure, the organization has an extendable platform to support additional districts and geographic areas as it grows. However, in order to implement Phases I and II, modifications to Bonnie CLAC Cars™ will be required. Section B below outlines these expected modifications.

2. QuickBooks

For its accounting and bookkeeping processes, Bonnie CLAC relies on another Intuit product, QuickBooks Nonprofit 2005 Premiere Edition. With over three million small business software customers and 230,000 accountants, QuickBooks is the #1 rated and recommended small enterprise financial management software.[77]

---

77 http://quickbooks.intuit.com/product/about-quickbooks/small-business-financial-software.jhtml

QuickBooks simplifies receiving funds, tracking expenses, making payments, and managing payroll. Data on clients, donors, vendors, and employees can be seen and tracked by Bonnie CLAC at a glance. At present, Bonnie CLAC makes limited use of QuickBooks' password-access and permissions features. As needed, Bonnie CLAC will make more extensive use of these features to limit users to specific data types and activities. Use of QuickBook's expanded permissions features and audit trail features will take Bonnie CLAC through Phases I and II of the business plan implementation.

B. Phase I Plan for Technology

Bonnie CLAC will engage a third party to review its long-term information technology needs. This review will be designed to answer several questions, including:

- How can any current deficiencies in Bonnie CLAC Cars™ be addressed most effectively and expeditiously?

- What new and/or revised functionality will be needed to support multi-district, multi-state, and national operations?

- Will QuickBase remain a cost-effective platform as operations grow?

- Will an intranet be needed to support internal operations and collaboration?

- Will additional hardware and/or software be required to support the business plan?

- Will additional staff, such as a Webmaster and/or a QuickBooks Administrator, be required to support Bonnie CLAC as it grows?

- Will QuickBooks Premier remain adequate or will Bonnie CLAC need to upgrade to QuickBooks Enterprise or Online Editions— or to another bookkeeping and accounting application?

Following this review, one or two technology partners will be selected to address Bonnie CLAC's short-term and long-term technological needs. In the short term, Bonnie CLAC will address deficiencies that might prevent the successful implementation of Phase I of the business plan. For the longer term, Bonnie CLAC will address any other technology issues identified by the third-party review so it will be poised for national rollout.

As part of its technology review, Bonnie CLAC will assess the functionality of Bonnie CLAC Cars™ as a scalable, national database system capable of handling both district and national operations; identify performance gaps in the system; and develop the additional features necessary to address these gaps. Such additional features may include the following (also listed in Bonnie CLAC Appendix 13 on page 173):

- Lifecycle tracking of data on prospects, clients, and alumni at each stage of the process

- Ability to summarize and report such data by day, week, month, and year

- Tracking, summarizing, and reporting on data by Client Consultant, office, district, (possibly) state, and national, with consistent comparative reporting across all entities

- Capture of standard data from prospects/clients, including referral source, reason for loss of prospect (if applicable), previous car, income and available income, and family size and type

- Use of drop-down selections wherever possible to ensure consistent data across the enterprise

- Transaction-based records, such that each transaction with a client is held as a separate record

- Alerts to remind Client Consultants to follow up with alumni after a set period or at other key times

- Ability to change sales stages over time

- Tracking of funding, donations, and in-kind contributions at the local, district, and national levels

- Reporting key-indicator data on dashboards for easy management access and action

VI. MARKETING

Phase I Goal: Establish the necessary marketing tools, programs, and partnerships for district and national expansion.

To carry out its district and national expansion, Bonnie CLAC plans to launch a dynamic marketing initiative consisting of three parts:

1. Develop a clear Brand & Communications strategy

2. Develop a target profile for successful Bonnie CLAC clients

3. Test three strategies to more effectively reach target clients

A. Brand & Communications
1. Brand

Bonnie CLAC will hire a Branding & Communications firm to develop a brand identity that clearly designates it as the organization that enables very low to moderate income individuals to purchase an affordable new car, which results in improvements in their lives and is consistent with maintaining a sustainable environment.

Upon completion of brand identity research, Bonnie CLAC and/or the Branding & Communications firm will formalize guidelines for logos and colors, create marketing templates for all communications efforts, and develop a consistent look, feel, and message across all marketing channels.

2. Communications

Bonnie CLAC will develop targeted messaging and produce the necessary communications materials to reach three core constituent groups—prospects, referrals, and local partners.

a. Bonnie CLAC will conduct historical research and survey best practices from both for-profit and nonprofit organizations in its industry to identify the key words, concepts, ideas, and images that resonate with prospects, referrals, and local partners.

b. Bonnie CLAC will conduct focus groups with each constituency to identify the most effective messages and communications materials for each group.

c. Bonnie CLAC will produce the necessary communications materials to broadcast its messages to its desired audiences.

The majority of Brand & Communications work will be done at the beginning of Phase I, with reviews and updates performed each subsequent year. The work will be led by the national office, in consultation with partners, constituents, Client Consultants, and other relevant parties, and disseminated through the district offices.

B. Target Client Profile

In order to scale its operating model, Bonnie CLAC will identify the most cost-effective and efficient ways to reach target clients in Phase I. The historical profile of a successful Bonnie CLAC customer is described below in Table I. This profile will be refined over time as additional data is collected.

Table I: Historical Profile of a Successful Bonnie CLAC Client

- Earns an average monthly income of ~$1900-$2200
- Has at least $300 in disposable income after monthly expenses are paid
- Has steady employment
- Is looking/willing to buy a new car
- Is/can learn to be fiscally responsible
- Does not have/is willing to work toward not having an account in collection

C. Target Marketing

Bonnie CLAC will test three strategies to more effectively reach its target clients: 1) referrals, 2) direct marketing, and 3) district partnerships. Bonnie CLAC will spend approximately $200 on marketing expenses for each successful car transaction in Year 1. The marketing budget will decrease to $175 per successful car transaction in Year 3 and $150 per successful car transaction in Year 5 (see Bonnie CLAC Appendix 14 for the Marketing Road Map).

1. Referrals

In Phase I, Bonnie CLAC will develop a systemic process to increase client referrals from a) Bonnie CLAC alumni, b) Bonnie CLAC employees, c) local small business and other district area organizations, and d) social service agencies.

a. Bonnie CLAC Alumni

Bonnie CLAC alumni (clients who have received their cars through successful completion of the Bonnie CLAC program) occasionally refer their friends and receive a one-time referral fee of $10 for each friend who enrolls in Bonnie CLAC and $25 for each friend who completes Bonnie CLAC. In Phase I, Bonnie CLAC will formalize both the process and the incentive system for alumni referrals (see Bonnie CLAC Appendix 15: Bonnie CLAC Alumni Membership Program on page 173).

b. Bonnie CLAC Employees

Bonnie CLAC employees and Board members have also made successful client referrals in the past. In Phase I, Bonnie CLAC will formalize both the process and the incentive system for employee referrals.

c. Local Small Business and Other District Area Organizations

Lead Client Consultants will identify local small businesses and other district organizations where employees can drop off promotional flyers tagged with location-specific codes (see Bonnie CLAC Appendix 16). These location-specific codes will be used to determine the district sites that provided the most and the best clients.

d. Social Service Agencies

Bonnie CLAC will continue to develop strong ties with local social service agencies in each district that work with its target client base. Lead Client Consultants will provide promotional flyers, deliver presentations, and maintain continuity of contact.

2. Direct Marketing

In addition to increasing referrals, Bonnie CLAC will pilot three direct marketing channels: a) direct mail, b) newspaper advertisements, and c) direct-mail coupon programs such as VAL-PAK. As it enters a new district or satellite location, direct marketing may be the most cost-efficient way for Bonnie CLAC to reach large numbers of target clients.

In each new district or satellite location, Bonnie CLAC will purchase contact information for local households that earn average monthly incomes of $1900 or above. Prospects who pass the initial income screen will be contacted by Bonnie CLAC via direct mail, newspaper advertisements, or direct-mail coupon programs such as VAL-PAK.

3. District Partnerships

Partnerships will play a critical role in Bonnie CLAC's growth and development. As Bonnie CLAC expands, it will continue to develop mutually beneficial partnerships with social service agencies, corporations, health organizations, and nonprofit organizations to recruit its target clients. Particular attention will be paid to regional and national entities that offer broad scaling opportunities.

a. Financial Fitness Organizations

In Phase I, Bonnie CLAC will pilot partnerships with social service agencies that teach high-quality financial fitness classes. Bonnie CLAC is currently testing a partnership with the Vermont chapter of JobCorps.

JobCorps Region One (http://bostonregion.jobcorps.gov) is a no-cost education and vocational training program administered by the US Department of Labor for young people ages 16 through 24 in Connecticut, Maine, Massachusetts, New Hampshire, New Jersey, New York, Rhode Island, Vermont, Puerto Rico, and the US Virgin Islands. One component of the JobCorps training program is a high-quality financial literacy class, which includes financial education, savings, and asset building.[78]

Bonnie CLAC has agreed to finance cars for select financial literacy graduates age 20 and above. If the partnership with the Vermont chapter proves successful, Bonnie CLAC will expand its partnership with JobCorps throughout New England and nationwide.

b. Corporations

Bonnie CLAC has initiated successful marketing campaigns with corporations in the New Hampshire district who employ a large number of workers fitting Bonnie CLAC's target demographic. These corporations publicize Bonnie CLAC's services internally to their employees; in return, Bonnie CLAC helps those employees who enroll in the program obtain more reliable transportation to get to and from work. In Phase I, Bonnie CLAC will develop a more formal corporate partnership package to standardize the way it solicits and partners with local corporations. (See Bonnie CLAC Appendix 17 on page 174.)

---

78 http://treasurer.delaware.gov/documents/2005/09-26-05-Financial_Literacy.shtml

c. Health Organizations

Bonnie CLAC will seek out organizations in the health industry as partners to help market its services. Health organizations know how much their clients and employees depend upon reliable transportation to obtain or provide health services. Many of their clients and employees also fit Bonnie CLAC's target demographic.

Dartmouth-Hitchcock Medical Center, located in Lebanon, NH, employs many successful Bonnie CLAC clients. Bonnie CLAC is currently developing marketing partnerships with other health-care organizations, such as The Edgewood Centre, a nursing and long-term care facility located in Portsmouth, NH.

d. Nonprofit Organizations & Universities

Bonnie CLAC will partner with nonprofit organizations and universities to recruit experienced and retired executives and college and business school students, respectively, as pro-bono marketing fellows who will work with Bonnie CLAC marketing personnel in creating marketing materials and implementing the organization's marketing strategy.

In the past, Bonnie CLAC has developed internships with United Way and Tuck Business School. United Way has a formal loaned executive volunteer program in which the United Way recruits local business executives and places them in community organizations in volunteer, marketing, training, account, and administrative management roles for a fixed period of time.[79]

In Phase I, Bonnie CLAC will partner with additional United Way chapters, business schools, and universities and develop a relationship with SCORE, an organization with 10,500 volunteer executives and business owners (both working and retired), who donate time and expertise as business counselors.[80] SCORE has 389 chapters throughout the United States and its territories. Using these partnerships, Bonnie CLAC will also develop a systematic volunteer recruitment and utilization process.

---

79 http://www.unitedwaycapitalarea.org/giving/le.cfm
80 http://www.score.org/explore_score.html

VII. STATE AND NATIONAL PARTNERSHIPS

Phase I Goal: Develop state and national partnerships that prepare Bonnie CLAC to scale.

In addition to the development of district partnerships, Bonnie CLAC will also develop mutually beneficial state and national partnerships with car manufacturers, financial institutions, and media outlets. In Phase I:

a. Bonnie CLAC will develop relationships with car manufacturers Honda and Toyota to obtain purchase discounts for its very low to moderate income clients.

b. To obtain loans for its clients nationwide, Bonnie CLAC will develop relationships with national financial institutions. Bonnie CLAC has identified the following banks as targets: Citizens Bank, Bank of America, Chase Manhattan Bank, and Citibank.

Bonnie CLAC's financial partners must:

- Be authorized to provide loans across the United States

- Offer wholesale interest rates to very low and moderate income clients if Bonnie CLAC serves as the guarantor

- Be willing to work with any Bonnie CLAC-approved client

- Be committed to the social vision of Bonnie CLAC. How active a financial institution has been in carrying out activities mandated by the federal Community Reinvestment Act (CRA) may serve as an indication of its commitment to Bonnie CLAC's social vision.

c. To increase press coverage of the organization's activities, Bonnie CLAC will develop strong partnerships with both local and national news media organizations.

(See Bonnie CLAC Appendix 18 on page 175 for a list of Bonnie CLAC's target district, state, and national partnerships.)

VIII. FINANCIAL SUSTAINABILITY

Phase I Goal: Bonnie CLAC will implement a financial sustainability strategy that builds profitable districts that will contribute financially to the national operational budget. As Bonnie CLAC strengthens its national operations, it will rely on a mix of earned and philanthropic revenues to support its growth.

Capitalization Required

Bonnie CLAC has already raised $1.2 million towards its growth strategy. Bonnie CLAC is now seeking an additional $2.7 million in Phase I and an additional $9.6 million in Phase II for a total capitalization of approximately $12.3 million over the next five years (see Table J). Approximately $4.3 million of the $12.3 million Bonnie CLAC is raising will go toward launching 25 new district offices.

As Table J below shows, Bonnie CLAC has also raised nearly $1.0 million in likely funds for Phase I. (See Appendix 19 on page 178 for a list of all of the philanthropic organizations that have made financial commitments to Bonnie CLAC for Phase I.) The Bonnie CLAC national office will also receive earned revenue contributions from the New Hampshire flagship district office in 2008 and from each new district office beginning in its third year of operations. In Phase I, Bonnie CLAC will also explore additional revenue stream opportunities with government agencies, corporate partners, and car manufacturers.

Table J: National Office Budget and Capitalization Required

	Phase I: 2008-2009	Phase II: 2010-2012
Total Expenses	$5,290,855	$20,429,965
Total Earned Revenues	$1,521,731	$10,743,530
Total Committed Funds Raised to Date	$1,060,500	$125,000
Total Capitalization Required	$2,708,624	$9,561,435
Total Likely Funds Raised to Date	$932,000	$0
Balance Remaining	$1,776,624	$9,561,435

Rest of Section Removed for Publication

Table K: New District Financial

Table L: Number of District Clients & Alumni

Table M: Required Pipeline Conversion Rates

Table N: Bonnie CLAC Program Fees

Table O: Number of New Hampshire Flagship District Clients & Alumni

Table P: New Hampshire District Financial Snapshot

Table Q: National Financial Snapshot

Figure I: Possible Bonnie CLAC 20-Year Financial Sustainability Trajectory (2007-2027)

IX. MEASUREMENT & QUALITY SYSTEM

Phase I Goal: Bonnie CLAC will develop the necessary dashboard(s) and processes to protect quality and establish a coordinated program to consistently measure organizational-health, program-performance, and social impact measurement in the areas of economic, health/lifestyle, and the environment.

Preliminary Results from Third-Party Evaluation of Social Outcomes

During the business planning process, The Carsey Institute at the University of New Hampshire conducted the first third-party evaluation of Bonnie CLAC's program outcomes. Final results on the social and economic impact of program participation in Bonnie CLAC will be published in a report in December 2007, with preliminary results described below.

The specific research questions posed by the study were:

- To what extent do participants' credit scores improve?

- To what extent do employment patterns and earnings change?

- To what extent does family/community involvement change?

- To what extent does overall well-being and health change?

The research consisted of in-depth interviews with 13 Bonnie CLAC alumni as well as questionnaire surveys sent to Bonnie CLAC alumni. A brief analysis of the interview data is included in the appendix. (See Bonnie CLAC Appendix 8 on page 155 for the interview guide and Bonnie CLAC Appendix 9 on page 158 for interview results.) The interviews provided insight into the impact of program participation, from overall improvement in "peace of mind" due to having a reliable automobile to improvements in job performance and budgeting. The interviews also provided data useful for the development of the survey instrument and the analysis of the survey data.

The survey (see Bonnie CLAC Appendix 10 on page 162) was sent to over 200 Bonnie CLAC alumni. Responses are still being received. The preliminary data on 48 responses received and coded to date show the following:

Although relatively few respondents have actually changed their jobs or earnings (10% and 17% respectively), getting to their jobs and doing so punctually have improved (48% and 38%).

Spending patterns have changed for many; respondents to date report spending less on gas (39%), insurance (27%), repairs (75%), and interest rates (42%). Many are also more careful about budgeting and paying their bills on time. These will do doubt lead to improved credit scores in the long run. The data on credit scores are still being obtained from lending institutions and will be analyzed when received.

Family and community involvement also appear to be affected by Bonnie CLAC participation: the majority of respondents report being better able to provide transportation for family members (56%), and many report improved ability to attend children's activities (33%). Almost half attend more community events, and three-quarters are in a better position to shop and run errands.

Finally, with respect to overall health and well-being, there are substantial improvements. Over half are better able to make health and dental appointments, and over a third have greater options for purchasing food and for health care. The majority of respondents report that their overall financial situation has improved (69%), and almost half are better able to pay their bills.

Although not one of the research questions, we also asked about satisfaction with the program; and not surprisingly, the vast majority of respondents to date report that their overall experience with Bonnie CLAC has been excellent (81%). Eighty-eight percent would recommend the program to others.

Indications are that the program is having the desired impact on clients with respect to community involvement and overall well-being. In addition, there is some evidence of job impacts, and spending patterns have changed dramatically. Given these findings from the survey, it is likely credit scores will show a positive change as well.

Implementing a Measurement and Quality System

Bonnie CLAC will measure the impact of its work by implementing three tasks:

A. Implement indicators

B. Implement measurement tools and tracking system

C. Implement feedback and self-evaluation

A. Implement Indicators

Bonnie CLAC will assess the status of its organization on an ongoing basis by implementing the following two types of indicators:
1) organizational-health and program-performance indicators and
2) social impact indicators.

Organizational-health and program-performance indicators provide critical insight into the stability of an organization, its capacity to carry out its work, and its relative success in accomplishing its business objectives. These indicators measure an organization's financial and operational health and performance. Each of Bonnie CLAC's organizational-health and program-performance indicators will be tied to one of the goals set forth in the various sections of this business plan.

For Bonnie CLAC, they will cover areas including consultant performance, marketing flow, financial performance, and partnership development. Such indicators will be reported at the district and national levels, as relevant.

They will also include measures of the organization's effectiveness in meeting its goals, such as building its national leadership team, its technological infrastructure, and its marketing programs. With few exceptions, such indicators will be relevant and reported only at the national level.

Bonnie CLAC's organizational health and program performance indicators appear below in Table R.

Table R: Bonnie CLAC Organizational-Health and Program-Performance Indicators

GOAL	INDICATOR
Goal 1: Establish profitable district offices in states nationwide	
DISTRICT	Consultant performance, % of capacity, by district
	Consultant performance, % of cars delivered, by district
	Prospect inquiries, % of target, by district
	Prospects screened, % of target, by district
	Clients enrolled, % of target, by district
	Cars delivered, % of target, by district
	Earned revenue, % of target, by district
	Philanthropic revenue, % of target, by district
	Expenses, % of target, by district
	Revenue/car, % of target, by district
	Expense/car, % of target, by district
	Average time from intake to car, by district
	Percent of clients in FastTrack, by district
	Percent of clients in BRIDGE, by district
	Percent of clients in FinFit, by district
	Number of Client Consultants, by district
	Number of cars available for BRIDGE, by district
	Number of clients on BRIDGE wait list, by district
	Bridge program bottom line
	Default rate, by district
	Districts by % of profitability
NATIONAL	Districts Opened
	Total Number of Districts
	Number of Clients Receiving Cars
	Amount of Financing Secured

Social impact indicators document an organization's progress in addressing its target social problem. For Bonnie CLAC, they will track the organization's effectiveness in improving the economic and health/lifestyle outcomes of its clients, and its impact on the environment.

In order to best develop a comprehensive list of social and economic indicators, Bonnie CLAC will continue working with experts to ensure they select the most commonly accepted indicators in improving the economic and health/lifestyle outcomes of its clients, and its impact on the environment. Below in Table S are the current list of Bonnie CLAC's social and economic impact indicators.

Table S: Bonnie CLAC Social and Economic Impact Indicators

Client credit scores on entry, graduation, and 6/12/18 months later (Goal SII 1)
Monthly wages on entry, graduation, and 6/12/18 months later (Goal SII 2)
Lengths of employment on entry, graduation, and 6/12/18 months later (Goal SII 3)
Disposable income on entry, graduation, and 6/12/18 months later (Goal SII 4)
Access to healthcare on entry, graduation, and 6/12/18 months later (Goal SII 5)
Gallons of gasoline used on entry, graduation, and 6/12/18 months later (Goal SII 6)
Carbon emissions on entry, graduation, and 6/12/18 months later (Goal SII 7)

B. Implement Measurement Tools and Tracking System

1. Organizational-Health and Program-Performance Indicators

The data needed to make measurements of the organizational-health and program-performance indicators will come from Bonnie CLAC Cars™ and QuickBooks, and from information and inquiries tracked by the Director of Measurement and Quality.

Wherever possible, the collection of the data needed to make measurements of the organizational-health and program-performance indicators will be integrated into Bonnie CLAC's organizational processes. These data will come primarily from Bonnie CLAC Cars™ and QuickBooks, and will be tracked automatically within those systems. As necessary, these applications will be modified to facilitate the collection, storage, tracking, and reporting of the indicators.

Other organizational-health and program-performance indicators will be developed by the Director of Measurement and Quality, primarily for those indicators that involve the tracking of milestones. The Director will gather such milestone data periodically from the managers responsible for the relevant programs and enter it into a tracking spreadsheet.

All organizational-health and program-performance indicators will be tracked and reported at district and/or national levels, as appropriate. They will be compared to budgets or targets, and will be viewable/re-portable by month, quarter, year, and prior year.

2. Social and Economic Impact Indicators

Securing the data needed to make measurements of the social and economic indicators will require baseline data from intake interviews, as well as surveys and/or interviews of alumni upon graduation, and 6, 12, and 18 months later. The surveys and/or interviews will be the responsibility of each alumnus' Client Consultant. The survey/interview data will be sent to the Director of Measurement and Quality for processing. The indicators will be tracked in a spreadsheet that will be designed for this purpose by the Director of Measurement and Quality. The Director will also create the dashboard needed for the feedback loop (see Section C below).

Social and economic impact indicators will be tracked and reported at the national level on a semi-annual basis by the Director of Measurement and Quality.

C. Implement Feedback and Self-Evaluation

1. Organizational-Health and Program-Performance Indicators

Bonnie CLAC will implement a process developed by the Director of Measurement and Quality to analyze the data for each of its organizational-health and program-performance indicators regularly and to apply such data to future decision making. On a monthly basis, The Director of Measurement and Quality will analyze these indicators and publish them as dashboards.

The dashboards will be designed by the Director of Measurement and Quality with the advice and consent of the Senior Management Team, They will be created for the district and national levels (with region-level summaries, if needed). Their form will depend on the nature of the data being reported, the ability of the organization's systems to produce reports in a final format, and the preferences of the Senior Management team. The dashboards might be simple spreadsheets; or, if management preferred, they could employ graphical images to enhance their display and use.

The CEO will review the district dashboards with his/her team and then with each Regional Director. The Regional Director (and possibly the CEO) will then review the district dashboards with each of that region's District Directors. Finally, each District Director will review relevant indicators with that District's Client Consultants.

The CEO will also review the national dashboard with Senior Management and other relevant national staff members.

The focus of all of these reviews will be to determine any issues and remedial actions required.

As appropriate, dashboards will include the following information:

- Goal

- Responsible individual

- Indicator

- Direction of change (>, <, =)

- Baseline

- Target

On an annual basis, the Director of Measurement and Quality will include relevant organizational-health and program-performance indicators in a report card of indicators to share with external stakeholders.

2. Social and Economic Impact Indicators

On a semi-annual basis, the Director of Measurement and Quality will analyze social and economic impact indicators and publish a dashboard (see Bonnie CLAC Appendix 23). Senior Management will review this dashboard to assess Bonnie CLAC's progress in achieving its social and economic goals. At these meetings, Senior Management will determine any issues and remedial actions required. Senior Management will also revisit Bonnie CLAC's Social Impact Model based on these indicators.

On an annual basis, the Director of Measurement and Quality will include relevant social and economic impact indicators in a report card of indicators to share with external stakeholders.

X. PUBLIC POLICY

Phase I Goal: Develop focused initiatives to support state and federal public policies that further the organization's mission and vision.

In Phase I, Bonnie CLAC will take a more proactive role in shaping public policy to support its mission and vision. According to the *Stanford Social Innovation Review*, high-impact nonprofits need to combine direct service programs with advocacy to reinforce and enhance their impact over time.[81] "High-impact organizations may start out providing great programs, but they eventually realize that they cannot achieve large-scale social change through service delivery alone." To have the greatest, long-term impact, Bonnie CLAC will focus on driving systematic change in the following four policy areas:

A. Transportation Individual Development Accounts (TIDA)

In recent years, Individual Development Accounts (IDAs) have become popular as an asset-building strategy for low-income individuals. IDAs are income-eligible savings accounts that are matched anywhere from a 1:1 to a 4:1 ratio from a combination of private and public sources.[82] The funds can be used for one of three purposes: i) education for the individual and/or children, ii) business capital, or iii) the purchase or repair of a home. Bonnie CLAC is in the early stages of developing a Transportation IDA (TIDA) to allow low-income individuals to save money toward the purchase of a new, reliable car.

---

81 McLeod Grant, Heather and Leslie R. Crutchfield (Fall 2007). "Creating High-Impact Nonprofits," Stanford Social Innovation Review, 5(3): 35. http://www.ssireview.org
82 http://www.hud.gov/offices/pih/programs/hcv/wtw/ppp/learning/nhFss.cfm

B. Temporary Assistance for Needy Families (TANF)

TANF was established in 1997 to provide assistance and work opportunities to needy families by granting states the federal funds and wide flexibility to develop and implement their own welfare programs. Citizens may apply for assistance at their local TANF agency. In the state of New Hampshire, TANF currently has an administrative regulation that prohibits TANF recipients from using their assistance to purchase cars worth more than $4000. Bonnie CLAC has begun work to change this regulation, so that TANF recipients can use their assistance to make down payments on new cars that are more reliable and cost efficient in the long run.

C. One-Time Earned Income Tax Credit (EITC)

The Earned Income Tax Credit (EITC), sometimes called the Earned Income Credit (EIC), is a refundable federal income tax credit for low-income working individuals and families. Bonnie CLAC is exploring the development of a one-time earned income tax credit to be used towards the purchase of a reliable, affordable car through a nonprofit organization.

D. Form Alliances

In Phase I, Bonnie CLAC will form alliances with government agencies, foundations, and other nonprofit organizations to focus on the most promising efforts to impact the organization's mission and vision. Bonnie CLAC will also conduct further research to identify additional public policy initiatives that could support its mission and vision.

Bonnie CLAC hopes to effect systematic change as it works toward the long-term goal that one day, very low to moderate income people will have broadly-available educational opportunities, a selection of reliable and affordable cars, and a variety of financing mechanisms to support the purchase of a car, all leading to improvements in their lives and to the environment.

XI. RISKS & EXTERNALITIES

Below are the four major risks associated with Bonnie CLAC's growth expansion and the steps Bonnie CLAC will take to mitigate them.

A. Hiring

As Bonnie CLAC expands, it will take intensive time and effort to recruit and hire the right executive for each national, regional, and district position. Excellent team-building dynamics will be crucial in executing the business plan in Phase I and longer term.

Mitigation: A search committee headed by Co-founder and Board Director Leo Hamill, and including both Bonnie CLAC's current President and Executive Director, has already been formed to find the CEO.

B. Focus

Bonnie CLAC will expand its operations using the criteria outlined in this business plan. Bonnie CLAC will focus on the mission, vision, and social outcomes stated herein, being careful to avoid mission creep and the distraction of focusing on too many social factors.

Mitigation: This business plan provides a detailed guide for Bonnie CLAC's expansion. The appendix section also provides more detail for immediate actions over the next six months in the form of a step-by-step action plan. If Bonnie CLAC carefully adheres to the action and business plans, it will be able to maintain its focus and accomplish its goals.

C. Marketing

Being able to find the right (target) clients and complete the required number of car transactions is crucial as each district office scales and moves toward profitability.

Mitigation: The business plan includes a robust marketing plan to be carried out by a dynamic Chief Marketing Officer. Marketing tests are already being conducted to determine the best course of action for Phase I.

D. Fundraising

Bonnie CLAC will need to raise nearly $12.3 million over the next five years to execute its business plan strategy.

Mitigation: Bonnie CLAC President Robert Chambers has already obtained almost $1.2 million in committed funds and nearly $1.0 million in likely funds from local, national, and government sources.

XII. ACTION PLAN

To begin implementation of Phase I, Bonnie CLAC will accomplish the following tasks outlined in the October 2007–March 2008 action plan:

ACTION PLAN (OCTOBER 2007–MARCH 2008)
Goal: To begin implementation of Phase I of the business plan, Bonnie CLAC will:
I) Organize and Strengthen the New Hampshire District
Reach marketing targets (See Appendix 24)
Re-organize New Hampshire District to emulate 'district model'
Re-organize New Hampshire District P & L to emulate 'district financial model' in b-plan and reach revenue and expense target
Begin testing of all three BRIDGE options
II) Prepare National Operations
Re-align positions between national and districts to start to emulate business plan
Hire CEO
Re-organize National P & L to emulate what is in the B-Plan and reach revenue and expense targets for 3 consecutive months
Develop action plan near completion of current action plan
Assess current team's time allocation and consider hiring additional support (i.e. PT development manager, contract CFO)
Target and begin meetings with primary target funders
III) Begin measurement and quality reporting system of NH District indicators that allows for feedback loop
Develop and execute monthly reporting system on some national indicators that allows for feedback loop
IV) Secure partnerships
Secure 1 corporate partnership to 'test' Bonnie CLAC value added in NH
Secure 1 partnership to test 'rent a wreck' option for BRIDGE cars in NH
V) Determine Best Area to Launch New District
Work with MIT Sloan team to develop district model roll-out plan

APPENDICES

Appendix 1—Bonnie CLAC Recognition and Awards

Awarded:

- The Purpose Prize
- The Manhattan Institute Award for Social Entrepreneurship

Media Coverage:

- *Time* Magazine
- *Business Week*
- *The Wall Street Journal*
- *The Washington Post*
- The Annie E. Casey Foundation newsletter

Major Donations and Grants from:

- The Byrne Foundation
- Community Development Finance Authority
- The Great Bay Foundation
- New Hampshire Charitable Foundation
- Norwin S. and Elizabeth N. Bean Foundation
- United Way of the Greater Seacoast

Contributions from:

- The Annie E. Casey Foundation
- Chicago Soft, Ltd.
- Chittenden Bank
- Citizens Bank
- Hanover Rotary Club
- Hypertherm Incorporated

- Johnson & Dix Fuel Corporation

- King Arthur Flour

- Ledyard National Bank

- Mascoma Savings Bank

- McLaughry Associates Inc.

- The Mountain

- Northeast Credit Union

- Ocean National Bank

- Page Hill Foundation

- Tele Atlas

- The Vermont Community Foundation

- The Women's Fund of New Hampshire

- Town of Hanover

- United Way of Merrimack County

- United Way of the Upper Valley

Appendix 2—Client Testimonials
Meet Robyn

Robyn had a job making $10 an hour while raising two little girls on her own. She had enough money to make a monthly car payment, and she hoped to take out a loan for a car. But Robyn had bad credit from a combination of credit card debt and a divorce. She was driving a 1993 Jeep that she had purchased for cash. The Jeep broke down frequently, and Robyn was about to lose her job because of tardiness and absences from work. Robyn was offered a loan at 25% interest rate on a 1999 Dodge Intrepid with 84,000 miles at a payment of $268 per month.

Robyn was about to buy this car. **Then she heard about Bonnie CLAC.**

When Robyn came to Bonnie CLAC, her expenses were analyzed by a Client Consultant. She was spending $277 per month on gas. If Robin drove a new fuel-efficient Toyota Corolla, her gasoline costs would drop to $104, **a savings of $173 per month**. She was also spending over $120 per month on car repairs. These unbudgeted repairs contributed to her credit card debt and caused her many absences from work.

After attending Financial Literacy, working on her budget, and repairing some credit items, Robyn was able to buy a new base model Toyota Corolla at a 6.4% interest rate with the help of Bonnie CLAC. Her car payment was $285 a month. This new car will still have five years of life after Robyn has finished paying for it. Until she found Bonnie CLAC, Robin did not have the information, negotiating skills, or access to credit necessary to make this purchase on her own.

Robyn cried when she got her new car because she was so excited. Robyn's credit has been restored, and she is now saving to buy a house, a lifelong dream that owning a reliable car helped to make possible.

Meet Jackie

Jackie worked 60 hours a week at three different part-time jobs while raising three young children on her own. She had enough money to make a monthly car payment, and she hoped to take out a loan for a car. But Jackie's credit was destroyed when her husband left her and her credit suffered during a divorce; she did not qualify for a loan and subsequently bought an old car for $2,000 cash.

In a month, the engine failed and Jackie had to walk to work. She spent $2,000 from her tax refund and her savings to replace the engine. Six months after that, the car's transmission died and Jackie traded in her car for $500 and bought a used car with a loan at a 25% interest rate. Six months later, it too broke down. Without a car, Jackie still had to make payments on her loan, and she walked to work two miles each way, often at night, until she found Bonnie CLAC.

With the help of the Financial Fitness classes, Jackie learned how to budget, manage her credit, take care of personal finances, and negotiate health care plans and car buying. When she felt ready, Bonnie CLAC guaranteed her low-interest loan for a new Honda Civic with a five-year bumper-to-bumper warranty. Jackie's payments were only $276 a month for the fuel-efficient, low-depreciating, reliable vehicle. Within two months of buying her new Honda Civic, Jackie found a higher paying job with health benefits. In addition, Jackie's credit score is now good enough that she is considering buying a house, something she says she never would have been able to do without Bonnie CLAC's assistance.

Appendix 3—Districts and Offices

New Hampshire District

- Lebanon, NH

- Keene, NH

- Manchester/Concord, NH

- Portsmouth/Exeter, NH

Appendix 4—Bonnie CLAC Pipeline Process

1. Recruiting

Bonnie CLAC recruits prospects from the very low to moderate income community. Local offices work with social service agencies to find prospective clients, partner with and make local company presentations, and distribute flyers to spread the word about Bonnie CLAC.

2a. Screening I:

After an initial inquiry comes in, Bonnie CLAC's Intake Manager uses a short, telephone-based survey to determine whether the prospect has at least $300 in disposable income after paying monthly expenses. This screening process helps ensure that those who come in for a Client Consultant interview have a good chance of enrolling and succeeding in the Bonnie CLAC program.

2b. Screening II:

Prospects who are approved over the telephone are invited to come to a local site and meet personally with a Client Consultant. They are asked to bring income and expense statements with them so the consultant can verify whether they have sufficient disposable income to meet monthly car, insurance, and gas payments. The goal of this meeting is to ascertain financial qualifications and to help prospects better understand the program so they can decide whether or not to enroll. Prospects who choose to enroll pay a $65 fee and become official Bonnie CLAC clients.

3. FastTrack or Counseling:

As soon as a client enters the program, the enrolling Client Consultant becomes his/her counselor. The Client Consultant works with the client to develop a customized plan that fits the client's personal financial status and situation. Clients with good to excellent credit records, stable employment, and residence history may enter FastTrack and receive a new car almost immediately. Otherwise, clients begin an intensive counseling program that includes credit repair, Financial Fitness (FinFit) classes, and other needed assignments required by the individual's profile.

- Credit Repair

Client Consultants perform one-on-one credit analysis to determine the credit counseling appropriate for each client. The customized clean-up plan is based on the client's credit history and his/her ability to make payments to creditors. Clients whose accounts are in collection can take 6-12 months to improve their credit history. During this time, Client Consultants will give clients "assignments" toward credit repair and (re)establishment of a positive payment history.

» Credit repair assignments may include paying charged-off loans, making plans to pay all regular monthly expenses (rent, utilities, loans, etc.) on time, explaining medical charge-offs, and identifying fraud or errors and correcting them.

» (Re)establishment of a positive payment history may include the creation of a savings plan and/or enrollment in Bonnie CLAC's transitional BRIDGE car program.

▫ During the savings plan, clients are required to deposit $250-$285 per month into a savings account, with the purpose of demonstrating their ability to build this recurring "expense" into their budget.

▫ The BRIDGE program provides clients who need a "bridge" loaner car with one at a cost of only $250 a month. At the same time, clients improve their credit records by building a history of on-time, monthly payments. The BRIDGE Manager places clients into this program, lines up the necessary BRIDGE cars for them, collects monthly payments, and conducts a review after two to three months. The BRIDGE Manager also helps transition BRIDGE clients into the next step of the program once their credit records have been sufficiently repaired.

- Financial Fitness (FinFit)

Financial Fitness (FinFit) is a five-week financial literacy program taught by a Bonnie CLAC FinFit Instructor. FinFit classes include budgeting and financial goal setting, checking-account management, money-saving techniques, protecting and building a positive credit history, and food economics and nutrition. Food economics and nutrition is included as a topic of Financial Fitness because Bonnie CLAC strives to help clients make economic shopping choices and improve health outcomes. Financial Fitness teaches clients to make sustainable changes in all aspects of their lives by encouraging personal growth related to self-worth and status, long-term planning and thinking, and the development of a healthy relationship to money.

4. Vehicle Selection:

The client and Client Consultant work together to select a vehicle that is appropriate for the client's budget, family size, and other needs. This selection is usually a Toyota Corolla or a Honda Civic, although other vehicles may be purchased with the approval of the Client Consultant. Bonnie CLAC's focus is on financing fuel-efficient cars. This goal helps combat fuel emissions and pollution even as it puts more very low to moderate income drivers on the road. Once a vehicle has been selected, the Client Consultant asks the Delivery Manager to locate the vehicle.

5. Financing a Car:

Upon completing the program and selecting a car, the client is now ready to purchase the car. The Client Consultant collects the following information in order to advocate for the client in his/her loan application.

- Client's length of time with Bonnie CLAC

- Programs completed with Bonnie CLAC (Credit Repair, Savings Plan, BRIDGE Program, Financial Fitness)

- Time at job

- Time at residence

- Current vehicle/transportation source

- Average weekly commute to work

- Explanation of credit issues

Bonnie CLAC enables its clients to obtain wholesale financing rates for their new car loans through partnerships with financial institutions. Bonnie CLAC acts as guarantor for the car loan. Interest rates average around 6.8%, which is exceptionally low for this particular client base.[83] Once the loan is submitted and approved by the financial institution, Bonnie CLAC's Delivery Manager completes the purchase and sale documentation and the bank loan paperwork necessary for the purchase of the new car. Clients sign a lease for a five-year loan, with monthly payments of $250-$285. Each client also pays a one-time loan guarantor's fee of $800 to Bonnie CLAC for financing and providing support throughout the duration of the loan. This $800 is built into the terms of the loan instead of coming directly out of the client's pocket.

6. Delivery of a New Car:

When the loan has been funded and the money has been paid to the car dealership, the Delivery Coordinator either accompanies the client to the local dealership to pick up the new car, or arranges for the local car dealership to drop it off.

7. Alumni Support:

Once Bonnie CLAC clients receive their new cars, they are known as Bonnie CLAC alumni. Bonnie CLAC alumni are contacted periodically by Client Consultants for follow-up and monitoring throughout the life of the car loan. This includes information or assistance with:

- Maintenance, repairs, warranties, and/or extended warranties

- Disputes with insurance companies over unfair claim decisions

- Communications with the financial institution regarding car loans

- Ongoing financial fitness support and education

- Discounts on new and used auto parts

- Preparations for future car purchases

---

83 Vogel, John H. Jr. (Marc 2005). "Bonnie CLAC Case Study." *Tucker School of Business at Darmouth*: 4.

Appendix 5—Social Impact Model

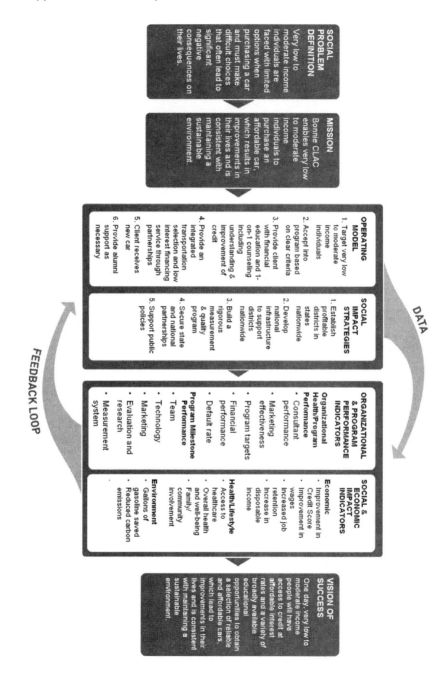

Appendix 6—Training Manual (Removed for Publication)
Bonnie CLAC Training Manual

Appendix 7—Selecting a District Site
Bonnie CLAC's district site selection will be guided by the following household, funder, and partner criteria.

I. State

    A. Determine which states within each region have the highest number of very low to moderate income households. (See Table H)

    B. Determine which states have the greatest fundraising capability.

    C. Determine which states have the greatest partnership support and potential.

II. City

In locating the district office within a qualifying state, Bonnie CLAC will use the following process:

    A. Use the US Department of Housing and Urban Development (HUD) guidelines and the US Census to determine the cities that have very low to moderate income populations of 120,000 households or more.

        1. Use the US Census to obtain the median household income for all metropolitan statistical areas (MSAs) in a given state. http://factfinder.census.gov/servlet/ADPGeoSearchByListServlet?ds_name=ACS_2005_EST_G00_&_lang=en&_ts=200697026088

        2. Use HUD guidelines (0–30% of the area median income = very low; 30–50% of the area median income = low; 50–80% of the area median income = moderate) and the US Census to calculate the total number of very low to moderate income households in all of the metropolitan statistical areas (MSAs) in that state.

        3. Identify the MSAs with at least 120,000 very low to moderate income households.

4. Because MSAs are usually calculated using a radius of 25 miles or less, it will often be necessary to pull additional data in order to qualify potential district sites. To do so:

   a. Identify the central zip code of the MSA.

   b. Locate zip codes within X miles of the central zip code, using (www.zip-code.com/zip-code-radius-finder.asp).

   c. Use the US Decennial Census to obtain the median household income for each zip code. http://factfinder.census.gov/servlet/DatasetMainPageServlet?_program=DEC&_submenuId=&_lang=en&_ts=

   d. Use HUD guidelines (0–30% of the area median income = very low; 30–50% of the area median income = low; 50–80% of the area median income = moderate) and the US Decennial Census to calculate the total number of very low to moderate income households in each zip code.

B. Determine which districts have the greatest fundraising capability. At a minimum, a district office must be able to raise $75,000 in start-up philanthropic funds to launch and an additional $50,000 in the next 18 months.

C. Determine which districts have the greatest partnership support and potential. Each district office must be supported by:

   1. Two or three social service and nonprofit referral agencies

   2. Two or three corporations that hire or serve a population fitting Bonnie CLAC's target profile

   3. At least one organization that can teach high-quality financial fitness classes

   4. At least one organization willing to provide in-kind office facilities for a start-up staff for the next two years

   5. One financing bank (if necessary)

D. Other criteria, such as distance to and from public transportation, centrality of location, or political considerations, may be taken into account at the discretion of the Regional Director and CEO.

Appendix 8—The Carsey Institute at the University of New Hampshire Third Party Evaluation Preliminary Interview Guide

Sample Interview Questions

Former Bonnie CLAC Participants (N=20)

1. How did you learn about Bonnie CLAC?

2. How did you become involved with Bonnie CLAC's programs?

3. Describe your involvement from the point of enrollment to a new car purchase.

4. Are there any aspects of your life that have changed since your participation in Bonnie CLAC's program?

Prods:

- Employment status

- Occupation

- Job training/education

- Community involvement

- Child's schooling/activities

- Health care (doctor/dental visits)

- Income

- Public assistance

- Credit

- Other

5. Do you know what your credit score was when you started the program?

6. What contributed to your credit status before participating in the program?

Prods:

- Credit card debt (any portion medical bills?)

- Medical debt

- Student loan debt

- Other debt

- Bankruptcy

- Foreclosure

- Unbanked status

- Other

- Don't know

7. How much has your participation in Bonnie CLAC's financial classes helped you manage your finances?

Prods:

- Debt

- Banked status

- Reallocation of finances; investment behavior

- Other

8. How much has your purchase of a new car through Bonnie CLAC helped with your economic position?

9. Would you change any aspects of the program? Please elaborate.

10. We would really like to see if your credit score has changed since your car loan through Bonnie CLAC. If we work with Bonnie CLAC to cover the cost of acquiring your score (it costs around $25), would you be willing to help us get your credit score?

The next questions are not as tied to your participation in the Bonnie CLAC program as the previous questions, but are interesting to us because adequate transportation might have implications for accessing health care, which is an important and timely topic given rising health care costs.

1. Are you, your spouse, and child(ren) covered by a health insurance plan?

2. Please describe the source(s) of your health insurance.

Prods:

- Employer sponsored

- Other private plan

- Medicaid

- Government

- Military

- Other

3. Have you ever struggled to afford your health insurance plan? Please elaborate.

4. Have you ever struggled with medical bills? Please describe.

5. Have actual medical bills ever impacted your finances?

Prods:

- Credit card usage

- Amount of savings

- Home purchase

- Educational attainment

- Ability to acquire loans

- Other investments

6. Has the threat of medical bills ever impacted your financial decisions?

7. Have actual medical bills ever impacted your employment?

Prods:

- Bills prevented R from getting needed health care, which hurt ability to work

- Work multiple jobs to afford medical bills

- Other

8. Has the threat of medical bills ever impacted your employment decisions?

Prods:

- Stayed in current job to ensure continuation of benefits

- Left current job for insufficiency of benefits

- Other

Appendix 9—The Carsey Institute at the University of New Hampshire Third Party Evaluation Preliminary Interview Results

Bonnie CLAC Interview Analysis

Carsey Institute

Fall 2007

Because of the sensitive nature of the questions being asked as part of the Bonnie CLAC Outcomes Research, the first step in the multi-method approach was to conduct interviews with a small sample of participants (N=13). This allowed the research team to learn about participants' experiences and perceptions regarding the program, which could then be used to inform the design of a survey instrument, to be sent to approximately 200 former Bonnie CLAC participants.

Following are a number of tables summarizing the responses from the interviews. It is important to keep in mind that only 13 observations were made. The distribution of answers may provide a sense of this sample's experiences but is not representative of all Bonnie CLAC participants. The value provided by the interviews was that the research team was able to put these answers in context based on other factors shared by respondents. Examples will be provided.

According to Table 1, most participants were either referred to Bonnie CLAC through an agency/nonprofit or by a friend, co-worker or family member (word of mouth).

Table 1. How Participant Became Involved with the Bonnie CLAC Program

How respondent heard of Bonnie CLAC	Freq.	Percent	Cum.
agency/org/nonprofit	4	30.77	30.77
word of mouth	5	38.46	69.23
newspaper/print	1	7.69	76.92
counselor	2	15.38	92.31
car dealership	1	7.69	100.00
Total	13	100.00	

One factor that emerged in the interviews that might be strongly related to whether or not a participant experiences economic changes in his/her life, especially in the short-term, is whether or not the participant had a car prior to joining the program. While "peace of mind" was frequently sited (see Table 4) as a benefit of the program, some participants who already had a car, albeit an unreliable car, experienced no immediate changes other than a reduction in fear about breaking down; however, they did hope that the overall experience would lead to an improvement in their credit over the long-term. Table 2 reveals that a large majority of those interviewed had cars prior to the program.

Table 2. Whether or Not Participants Had a Vehicle Prior to the Program

The Respondent's car situation	Freq.	Percent	Cum.
no car	4	30.77	30.77
unreliable car	9	69.23	100.00
Total	13	100.00	

As might be expected, almost all of the participants interviewed struggled with credit and/or a lack of income, which led to their participation in the program. A factor that emerged from these answers as something for consideration includes reasons for bankruptcy. For instance, one respondent had filed due to divorce. The respondent claimed that she had no credit cards, but that she inherited part of her ex-spouse's debt, which for her was "inconceivable". From this participant's standpoint, a change in credit score may be her biggest goal and job changes would not apply. Another respondent had filed due to an investment in a business venture, which he did on the side of his steady job. After utilizing credit cards to fund his investment, the respondent found himself consumed in debt. Again, this respondent's income and job are unlikely to change, but there is still potential for an impact, especially with his credit score over the long-term.

These examples reveal that in some cases, participants may not show impacts in certain areas despite dire circumstances at the onset but that impacts could occur in other areas. Two interviewees who cited bankruptcy as a factor described how the program affected them in ways that are not tied to job changes. These interviews suggest the importance of looking at a range of outcomes of the program.

Table 3. Reason Why Participant Needed Bonnie CLAC's Help

The reason the respondent needed Bonnie CLAC	Freq.	Percent	Cum.
no/poor credit and low income	5	38.46	38.46
poor credit	3	23.08	61.54
bankruptcy	4	30.77	92.31
wanted guidance	1	7.69	100.00
Total	13	100.00	

When asked about what changes respondents experienced after the program, peace of mind was cited repeatedly. This of course, may be a function of the large proportion of people in this sample who had an unreliable car prior to going through the program. Other respondents mentioned multiple positive changes as indicated in Table 4. One factor that emerged from these answers is the role that age may play in a participant's experiences.

A participant that experienced positive changes in her job and her living situation admitted that the changes were due to the fact that she was graduating from college and moving out of her parent's home for the first time. Her participation in the program coincided with these milestone events. This is not to say that the program did not help her in numerous ways—she had a lot of debt and needed guidance—but that without this knowledge, one might assume that her job and living changes resulted from the program as opposed to her personal development.

Table 4. Positive Changes Experienced After the Bonnie CLAC Program

Changes experienced by the respondent after the program	Freq.	Percent	Cum.
peace of mind	4	36.36	36.36
job performance	2	18.18	54.55
budget, transport fam, & invest	1	9.09	63.64
peace of mind, job, & invest	1	9.09	72.73
peace of mind, job, & transport fam	1	9.09	81.82
budget, job, & invest	1	9.09	90.91
budget, job, & transport fam	1	9.09	90.91
Total	11	100.00	

Interviewees were asked about suggestions for improvement, summarized in the last table. Regardless of these suggestions, every single respondent had positive feelings about the Bonnie CLAC program and seemed grateful for the experience. Several respondents mentioned referring other friends and family and some said they had purchased more than one car through Bonnie CLAC. When asked how Bonnie CLAC could improve its services, respondents shared suggestions listed in Table 5. Some individuals had to really think about an answer, but one suggestion that 3 participants felt strongly about was that there should be more car options.

Table 5. Suggestions for Improving Bonnie CLAC's Services

Suggestions for improvement to the program	Freq.	Percent	Cum.
no suggestion	3	3.08	23.08
provide follow up	2	15.38	38.46
more car options	3	23.08	61.54
make loaner cars cheaper	1	7.69	69.23
reduce fee	2	15.38	84.62
fix paperwork issues	1	7.69	92.31
more assistance with credit	1	7.69	100.00
Total	13	100.00	

Summary

Based on the preliminary interviews, it is obvious that while many participants share a status of poor credit and/or a lack of income, their situations vary tremendously. Some individuals admitted to struggling persistently, while others had been hit more recently. Participants also shared gratitude toward Bonnie CLAC, and multiple respondents said something to the extent of having no idea what they would have done without Bonnie CLAC's assistance.

The interviews provided insight into what factors might be important for the survey design but also for analyzing the survey data. There are certainly instances when what appear to be impacts might be something else like personal development and other instances when a lack of observable impacts in one area does not necessarily mean the participant was not affected in other ways.

Appendix 10—The Carsey Institute at the University of New Hampshire Third Party Evaluation Final Survey Instrument

This survey will provide important information about Bonnie CLAC and how it helps clients. Your participation is completely voluntary. You will receive a $10 gift card along with your current credit score once we receive the signed release and completed survey.

Please fill this out now and return the survey and signed release form in the self-addressed, stamped envelope. This survey is important for Bonnie CLAC. Please accept our sincere thanks.

Please circle the number of your response or fill in the blank. Thank you!

Your Situation Before Bonnie CLAC

1. Which of the following describes your situation before you went through Bonnie CLAC?

    1. I did not have a car

    2. I had an unreliable car

    3. My family needed a second car

    4. Other _____

2. What are the reasons that you went through Bonnie CLAC (circle all that apply)?

   1. Poor credit

   2. Needed a bridge car

   3. Needed budget/financial counseling

   4. Wanted assistance working with a car dealer

   5. Needed assurance that I could afford car payments

   6. Had no money to put down

   7. Other _____

Changes Since Participating In The Bonnie CLAC Program

3. Which of the following activities have you been able to do as a result of completing the Bonnie CLAC program (circle all that apply)?

   1. Finding a job

   2. Getting to my job

   3. Going to health/dental care appointments

   4. Having more options for food

   5. Having more options for health care

   6. Participating in schooling/training programs

   7. Transporting family members

   8. Attending child's activities (sporting events, plays, etc.)

   9. Accessing day care

   10. Attending community events

   11. Shopping/running errands

   12. Other_____

4. Going through the Bonnie CLAC program has helped me accomplish the following job changes (circle all that apply):

    1. I found a new job

    2. I found a better job

    3. I found a better paying job

    4. I can work a steady schedule

    5. I arrive on time for work

    6. I have received a pay increase in my current job (hourly wage increase of: $_____)

    7. I work more hours per week (approximately _____ more hours per week)

    8. I receive better benefits (health insurance, retirement, life insurance, etc.)

    9. Other_____

    10. No changes in my job situation due to Bonnie CLAC

5. Due to your participation in Bonnie CLAC's program how has your spending changed (circle all that apply)?

    1. I spend less on gas for my car

    2. I spend less on insurance for my car

    3. I spend less on repairs for my car

    4. I spend less on interest rates

    5. I am more careful about my purchases

    6. I am more likely to pay bills on time

    7. I have less pressure from creditors

    8. Other_____

6. How has your overall financial situation changed since you purchased your car? Is it

   1. much better

   2. somewhat better

   3. no different

   4. worse

7. Due to your experience with Bonnie CLAC, which of the following aspects of your overall financial situation have changed (circle all that apply)?

   1. I have more money at the end of each month (approximately $_____ more per month)

   2. I am better able to pay my bills

   3. I put money into my savings account

   4. I put money towards a rainy day fund and/or a reserve for emergencies

   5. I am saving to buy a home

   6. I am investing in a small business

   7. I am investing in a retirement account

   8. I am able to afford better recreational activities

   9. I have been able to put money aside for education

   10. I am able to afford more nutritious food

   11. Other (please explain)_____

8. Do you currently have health insurance?

   1. yes   2. no

9. Did you have health insurance before your experience with Bonnie CLAC?

   1. yes   2. no

Your Feelings About Bonnie CLAC

10. Please rate your overall experience with Bonnie CLAC

   1. excellent   2. good   3. fair   4. poor

11. If a friend or relative needed a new car, would you recommend that they work with Bonnie CLAC to obtain a new car?

   1. Definitely yes   2. Maybe   3. Definitely no

   Please explain: _____

   _____

12. During your experience with Bonnie CLAC, what three things were the most important to you?

   1. Access to a bridge car

   2. Financial literacy class

   3. Consulting services

   4. Help with the car loan

   5. Knowledge about the car industry

   6. Knowledge about how to find and keep a job

   7. Other, please specify _____

13. Is there anything else you would like to tell us about your experience with Bonnie CLAC?

Finally, Some Questions About You and Your Background

14. Are you male or female?

   1. Male   2. Female

15. What is your age? _____ years old

16. What is your marital status?

   1. married   2. single   3. divorced/separated   4. other

17. How many children do you have under the age of 19?_____

18. How far did you go in school?

   1. Less than high school

   2. High school diploma or GED

   3. Some college

   4. Associate's Degree

   5. Bachelor's Degree

   6. Graduate/Professional Degree

   7. Other_____

19. Are you currently employed?

   1. yes   2. no

If you are willing to be interviewed by a researcher of health insurance at UNH, about your experiences with medical bills, please provide your first name and number. If you are not willing, leave it blank.

First name _____

Preferred Number _____

THANK YOU FOR COMPLETING THIS SURVEY. WE WILL SEND YOUR $10 GIFT CARD AND YOUR CREDIT SCORE WITHIN A FEW DAYS OF RECEIVING THE COMPLETED SURVEY AND RELEASE FORM.

PLEASE RETURN THIS SURVEY AND THE SIGNED RELEASE IN THE ENCLOSED SELF-ADDRESSED, STAMPED ENVELOPE. THANK YOU!

Appendix 11—Biographies of Board of Directors and Advisory Board

Merilynn Bourne; Cornish, NH (advisory member)

Executive Director of LISTEN Community Services; extensive background in administration, marketing and personnel management with many years of retail experience; living in Cornish, NH; member of the Finance Committee, the PTO, the Cornish Fair Association; and Assistant Town Moderator for five years.

Mary Burnett; Hinsdale, NH

Executive Director of Bonnie CLAC; 28 years experience in retail car industry as Dealer Principal; ongoing Volunteer Instructor for the Bonnie CLAC Financial Fitness program, as well as periodic guest speaker at community and educational events.

Robert Chambers; Hanover, NH

President and Co-Founder of Bonnie CLAC; Major Gifts Development Officer with Dartmouth-Hitchcock Medical Center; E-Commerce Manager, Miller Automobile; fundraiser for River Valley Club; President and founder of Computer Software Company in New York, NY; Vice President Sales Dartmouth subsidiary, DTSS Inc. Robert worked as an auto salesman for four years and became ever more disillusioned with how low-income individuals were treated when they purchased a car. These individuals were frequently sold older cars because they were more profitable to the dealers, at high interest rates and with terms that the buyer did not understand. The culminating experience came when Robert saw the sales person and the business manager celebrate with a "high-five" when they completed a sale to a vulnerable low-income single mother. The sale resulted in a $5,000 profit. Robert decided something had to change; so began Bonnie CLAC.

Allan Ferguson; Meriden, NH

Robert E. Field, Sr.; Hanover, NH

Retired Deputy Chairman, Price Waterhouse; Trustee Dartmouth College; Treasurer of Dartmouth College; Chairman Board of Overseers Tuck School of Business; Trustee and Chairman of Dartmouth-Hitchcock Medical Center; Named Fiduciary of the JP Morgan Chase Bank Employee Benefits Plans.

Beth Ann Finlay; Northfield, VT (advisory member)

Executive Director of Northern Vermont Research Conservation and Development Council.

Leo Hamill, Jr.; Hanover, NH

Co-Founder of Bonnie CLAC; Vice President, Sales, Miller Automobile; General Sales Manager, Miller Nissan Jeep; Superintendent of Highways, Town of Hanover; Projects Manager Northland Real Estate

Development Co.; Director of Public Works, Bridgeton, ME.; Member of the Hanover Lions Club for 12 years.

Robert G. Hansen; Hanover, NH

Senior Associate Dean and Norman W. Martin 1925 Professor of Business Administration at the Tuck School of Business at Dartmouth College, where he has been on the faculty since 1983. Professor Hansen oversees academic areas of the Tuck School, including faculty recruiting, promotion, and research matters.

David Reeves; Norwich, VT

Ph.D. from Harvard University; a private investor in the financial markets; Professor, McCormick Theological Seminary in Chicago, locally active in school and nonprofit organizations.

Judith Richard; Concord, NH

Judith has over 30 years of experience in corporate real estate and more than seven years experience in the New Hampshire real estate market. She holds degrees in Accounting and Marketing from Franklin Pierce College and a Masters Certificate in Human Resources from Southern NH University Graduate School of Business. Judith is the 2006 president of the Women's Council of Realtors and the recipient of the 2006 Realtor Member of the Year Award from the Central NH Women's Council of Realtors and the Women's Council of Realtors, State of New Hampshire. In addition, she is the Vice President of Administration for the Silverstein Organization.

Chandra L. Ribiero; West Lebanon, NH. (Bonnie CLAC Client Representative)

Rick Sayles, CPA, CFA, CFP; Hanover, NH

Owner of a financial consulting business. Active in several non-profit organizations. Background experience at Price Waterhouse and Prudential Insurance.

Appendix 12—Chief Executive Officer Job Description

Bonnie CLAC is a 501(c) (3) founded in 2001. Bonnie CLAC's mission is: to help low and moderate-income individuals buy new fuel efficient vehicles. Bonnie CLAC provides a partial guarantee of the loans, extensive counseling services and teaches a Financial Literacy Course that helps clients to become successful and economically self-sufficient. Bonnie CLAC has received a grant to expand our program and services into three additional states in New England. We are also working on a strategic business plan for a National Expansion. For more information, please visit www.bonnieclac.org, or Contact:

Robert Chambers, President (603) 727-7006.

Position:

Bonnie CLAC has been growing steadily and is now seeking to dramatically accelerate its growth. The Board and President are looking for a mission-focused, seasoned, strategic, and process-minded leader with experience scaling an organization, leading an executive management team, and developing a performance culture among a group of diverse, talented individuals. The CEO must be a leader who is able to help others at the Organization deliver measurable, cost-effective results that make the vision a reality. Importantly, the successful CEO will have the skills, sensitivity, and personal confidence to tap into the power that each member of the team brings to this mission. While it is essential that the CEO bring efficient and effective systems to increase the productivity of the Organization, is it also critical that the team retain the creative spark that drives the BONNIE CLAC concept and vision.

Responsibilities

Working in partnership with the President of Bonnie CLAC, the CEO will lead all internal operations and will have the following responsibilities:

- In partnership with the President, implement the strategic five-year plan and implement new processes and approaches to successfully achieve it.

- Serve as the internal leader of the organization:

  » Coordinate the annual operations plan and budget

  » Lead the performance management process that measures and evaluates progress against goals for the organization

» Provide for all staff a strong day-to-day leadership presence; bridge national and regional operations and support an open-door policy among all staff

- Hire, lead and manage the organization's senior level managers who have the following responsibilities:

  » New site development

    ▫ Raise local funds

    ▫ Build local fund raising communications and Client Consulting infrastructures within local offices

    ▫ Generate sufficient local revenue to cover local costs

    ▫ Identify geographic growth opportunities and priorities

    ▫ Communicate the branded message internally and externally

  » Program

    ▫ Increase key impact measurements

    ▫ Ensure that all programmatic partners renew their contracts

    ▫ Develop curriculum, tools, and training that meet cost guidelines

Bonnie CLAC currently has four fully operational offices in New Hampshire and will open eight additional offices in four New England States over the next two years.

Key Qualifications

As a prerequisite, the successful candidate must believe in the core values of BONNIE CLAC and be driven by the mission. The candidate should demonstrate a passion for breaking new ground to lead social change. Beyond that, we are seeking a candidate that has proven experience in scaling a multi-site organization and a demonstrated ability to both lead and build the capabilities of a driven, bright, diverse team.

The successful candidate will most likely have had management experience with a for-profit organization. As noted, this is an organization driven by the values of its people, so experience in managing a "values-driven" organization will be highly prized. Additional requirements are:

- Results—proven track record of exceeding goals and a bottom-line orientation; evidence of the ability to make good decisions through a combination of analysis, wisdom, experience, and judgment; high level of business acumen, including successful P&L management and the ability to balance the delivery of programs against the realities of a budget; problem solving, project management, and creative resourcefulness

- Strategic Vision and Agility—ability to think strategically, anticipate future consequences and trends, and incorporate them into the organizational plan

- Capacity Building—ability to effectively build organization and staff capacity, developing a top-notch workforce and the processes that ensure the organization runs smoothly

- Leadership and Organization—exceptional capacity for managing and leading people; a team builder who has experience in scaling up organizations; ability to connect staff both on an individual level and in large groups; capacity to enforce accountability, develop and empower top-notch leaders from the bottom up, lead from the top down, cultivate entrepreneurship, and learn the strengths and weaknesses of the team so as to put people in a position to succeed

- Action Oriented—enjoys working hard and looks for challenges; able to act and react as necessary, even if limited information is available; not afraid to take charge of a situation; can overcome resistance to leadership and take unpopular stands when necessary

- General Management—thorough understanding of finance, systems, and HR; broad experience with the full range of business functions and systems, including strategic development and planning, budgeting, business analysis, finance, information systems, human resources, and marketing

- Solid Educational Background—undergraduate degree required; MBA or similar advanced degree highly desired

Compensation

This is an outstanding opportunity for a highly motivated professional to assume a pivotal role in the evolution of a fast-growing, highly respected organization. We are seeking an individual of outstanding quality with a respected track record. Bonnie CLAC is prepared to offer a very attractive compensation package, including a competitive base salary.

Appendix 13—Bonnie CLAC Cars™ System Functions

Bonnie CLAC Cars™ performs the following functions:

- Inbound client call management

- Initial telephone profile intake and client registration

- Financial fitness course registration

- Counseling session logging

- Appointment and class scheduling

- BRIDGE car recordkeeping

- Donation acceptance

- Correspondence creation and tracking

- Car dealer relations

- Loan processing, including preparation and storage of loan documentation

- Title transfers

- Summarizing and reviewing operational activities

Appendix 14—Marketing Road Map
(Removed for Publication)

Appendix 15—Bonnie CLAC Alumni Membership Program

Objective: Bonnie CLAC will maintain ongoing relationships with clients and enhance their connection to the organization by offering valuable car-related services and continued assistance with financial and car-related matters. In return, Bonnie CLAC will solicit referrals from alumni members and consider the charge of a small annual fee to cover the Client Consultant salary.

Potential Benefits:

- Newsletter

- Alerts regarding scams

- Financial and other tips

- Ongoing educational opportunities

- Roadside assistance through AAA partner

- Other discounts and coupons

- Support group

- Social events

Potential Payment Options

- Additional $5 a month on loan

- Annual membership fee

- Sponsorship underwritten by AAA, financial institutions, insurance agencies, etc.

Appendix 16—Sample Promotional Flyer (Removed for Publication)

Appendix 17—Corporate Partnership Package

Bonnie CLAC will develop partnerships with corporations that fit the following profile:

1. A significant number (> 50%) of the company's employees qualify as low wage workers.

2. The company is large enough (usually > 60 employees) to have a full-time human resources coordinator.

3. The company is growing or experiencing employee turnover. It might also be experiencing problems with recruitment.

4. The company offers employee benefits.

5. The company requires travel as part of the job for some of its employees.

Bonnie CLAC will test the use of the Corporate Partnership Package with its corporate partners. This package consists of:

- Paycheck stuffers

- Break room posters

- Newsletter article series to be placed in the company newsletter

- Lunch-and-learn presentations, including a DVD with the Bonnie CLAC PBS segment

Appendix 18—Target Partnerships

CURRENT PARTNERSHIPS	FUTURE PARTNERSHIPS
Targeted local small businesses	Local small businesses
• Irving Oil	• mom & pop tire shops
	• repair shops
	• gas stations
	• day cares
	• hair dressers
	• women's gyms
Social service agencies	Social service agencies
• ACORN	• JobCorps

- Aids Project of Southern VT
- ALANA Community Services
- Alice Peck Day Community Hospital
- American Red Cross
- Area Agency on Aging
- CATCH
- Cheshire Housing Trust
- CCCS
- Families in Transition
- Good Beginnings
- Good New Garage
- Granite State Independent Living
- HCRS
- Keene Housing
- Listen
- MCRC
- Michael's House
- Micro Credit of NH
- Monadnock Development Services
- NH Employ Security
- NH Minority Health Coalition
- Service link
- SEVCA
- SCS
- Upper Valley Ride Share

- Housing coalitions

Corporations	Corporations
- Hypertherm	- See profile in Appendix 17

Health organizations	Health organizations
- Dartmouth-Hitchcock Medical Center	- Northern New England LEADS Institute

- The Edgewood Centre
- Endowment for Health
- Hospitals
- Nursing homes
- Health care agencies

Nonprofits/universities	Nonprofits/universities
- United Way - Tuck Business School	- United Way - SCORE - Business schools and universities throughout the country - Adult education institutes

Local car dealerships	National car manufacturers
- Toyota of Keene - Honda of Keene - Subaru of Keene - Fairfield's Motors - Berlin City Auto - Autex of Keene - Gerrish Motors	- Honda - Toyota **Car rental companies** - Enterprise - Avis - Budget - Alamo - National - Dollar - Thrifty - Hertz - Rent-a-Wreck

Financial institutions	Financial institutions
- Chittenden Bank - Northeast Credit Union	- Citizens Bank - Bank of America - Chase Manhattan Bank - Citibank

Local & national news media	Local & national news media
• PBS	• To be determined
• *BusinessWeek*	
• *Time*	
• *The Wall Street Journal*	
• *The Washington Post*	

Government agencies	Government agencies
• State of New Hampshire	• Local agencies
• CDFA	• State agencies
	• Federal agencies

Funding organizations	Funding organizations
• The Annie E. Casey Foundation	• Robert Wood Johnson Foundation
• The Great Bay Foundation	• Jane's Trust
• The Endowment for Health	• Skoll Foundation
	• N.H. Charitable Fund
	• The Byrne Foundation
	• Bean Foundation
	• Page Hill Foundation
	• Betterment Fund

Targeted Philanthropic Organizations

Local Foundations

- The Byrne Foundation
- New Hampshire Charitable Fund
- Page Hill Foundation
- Endowment for Health
- Neil & Louise Tillotson Foundation
- Betterment Fund (Maine)

Government

- Federal Government Earmark

Appendix 19—Committed and Targeted Philanthropy (Removed for Publication)

Appendix 20—National Financial Model and Notes (Removed for Publication)

Appendix 21—District Start-up Financial Model and Notes (Removed for Publication)

Appendix 22—New Hampshire District Model and Notes (Removed for Publication)

Appendix 23—Social and Economic Indicator Dashboard (Removed for Publication)